12.95

UNOFFICIAL AND UNAUTHORIZED—
THE COMPLETE STORY!!!

America's favorite TV spies!

The
U.N.C.L.E.
TRIBUTE BOOK

ROBERT ANDERSON

(800) 444-2524 Ext 67

PIONEER BOOKS

MTV: MUSIC YOU CAN SEE   ISBN#1-55698-355-7
TREK: THE NEXT GENERATION CREW BOOK   ISBN#1-55698-363-8
TREK: THE PRINTED ADVENTURES ISBN#1-55698-365-5
THE CLASSIC TREK CREW BOOK   ISBN#1-55698-368-9
TREK VS THE NEXT GENERATION   ISBN#1-55698-370-0
TREK: THE NEXT GENERATION TRIBUTE BOOK ISBN#1-55698-366-2
THE HOLLYWOOD CELEBRITY DEATH BOOK   ISBN#1-55698-369-7
LET'S TALK: AMERICA'S FAVORITE TV TALK SHOW HOSTS   ISBN#1-55698-364-6
HOT-BLOODED DINOSAUR MOVIES ISBN#1-55698-365-4
BONANZA: THE UNOFFICIAL STORY OF THE PONDEROSA   ISBN#1-55698-359-X

EXCITING NEW TITLES SOON TO BE RELEASED

THE KUNG FU BOOK   ISBN#1-55698-328-X
TREK: THE DEEP SPACE CELEBRATION   ISBN#1-55698 330-1
MAVERICKS: TV'S WESTERN HEROES   ISBN#1-55698-334-4
TREK: THE DEEP SPACE CREW BOOK   ISBN#1-55698-335-2
MARRIAGE & DIVORCE -HOLLYWOOD STYLE   ISBN#1-55698-333-6
THE LITTLE HOUSE COMPANION   ISBN#1-55698-332-8
TREK: THE NEXT GENERATION TRIBUTE BOOK TWO ISBN#1-55698-329-8
TREK: THE ENCYCLOPEDIA   ISBN#1-55698-331-X

COVER BY MORRIS SCOTT DOLLENS

Library of Congress Cataloging-in-Publication Data
Robert Anderson, 1993—

The U.N.C.L.E. Tribute Book

1. The U.N.C.L.E. Tribute Book (television, popular culture)
I. Title

First Printing, 1994

Publisher and Designer: Hal Schuster   **Editor: David Lessnick**

CONTENTS

THE UNCLE TRIBUTE

DEDICATION

TO
Napoleon and Illya

The U.N.C.L.E. TRIBUTE BOOK

America's favorite TV spies!

Introduction

Back to the Sixties

When the MAN FROM U.N.C.L.E. premiered in September 1964, it hit at exactly the right time. Ever since the first James Bond film, DR. NO, had been released in 1962, and President Kennedy mentioned that he enjoyed reading the James Bond novels, a spy craze had been building in the entertainment field. In 1963 Norman Felton pitched the original concept for U.N.C.L.E. to NBC and when the series began airing in 1964 it was at the peak of the James Bond boom immediately following the release of GOLDFINGER.

But while U.N.C.L.E. was inspired by Bond, it wasn't an imitation. U.N.C.L.E. has its own individual style and approach. While Bond is a loner, Solo and Kuryakin are the perfect espionage team and their adventures are even more far flung than James Bond's are.

U.N.C.L.E. made use of cutting edge ideas involving technology and told stories involving cunning as well as suspense. In spite of being a product of the sixties, the best U.N.C.L.E. adventures don't come across as being nailed down to their time (except for the worst ones). U.N.C.L.E. was at its best when it was trying to tell intelligent, exciting stories. It was at its worst when it tried to imitate what worked for someone else. When U.N.C.L.E. innovated, it flew. When it imitated, it crashed and burned.

If I had to recommend what episodes to watch I'd say any from the first season (the black and white year) and the fourth season. But U.N.C.L.E. never died.

Like STAR TREK, interest in the series remained. The U.N.C.L.E. books actually continued for a couple years after the series ended because the die-hard fans kept buying them. Some fans tried to get a feature film off the ground in the late '70s and early '80s, as is chronicled in detail in this book. And THE FIFTEEN YEARS LATER AFFAIR did appear in 1983, and that is examined here as well.

On the historical front we feature some items which have never appeared in a book before. There is the original U.N.C.L.E. premise, still titled "SOLO," which was pitched to NBC at the time the pilot was filmed. There is also the original GIRL FROM U.N.C.L.E. premise which was pitched to NBC at the time of "The Moonglow Affair," and before the network told the producers to recast the characters.

Today there is serious talk of a new U.N.C.L.E. movie which may well relaunch the series popularity all over again. There are many reasons why the '90s have been called a return to the '60s and a re-examination and revival of the favorite shows of that era are a prime example, of which U.N.C.L.E. was clearly on the cutting edge.

—JAMES VAN HISE

It was 1962. The height of what would come to be known as the "James Bond boom" was still two years away, and yet a producer was already anticipating this and planning to capitalize on it.

Chapter One
THE BIRTH OF U.N.C.L.E

The early sixties were the period of two great crazes. One was known as Beatlemania, and the other could best be described as Spy Fever. Both had their origins in England, as the Spy Craze was largely an offshoot of Ian Fleming's James Bond novels, published in the fifties and made into the highly successful Bond film series. Cold war tensions heightened interest in espionage, but most spy stories were more concerned with action and sex than with political considerations. A notable exception is the work of John LeCarré, whose novels explored the moral ambiguities of the secret agent's dark existence. The movie version of THE SPY WHO CAME IN FROM THE COLD is a true classic.

THE MAN FROM U.N.C.L.E. did not examine such issues, but tackled the Bondian basics with a style and wit of its own. Some were quick to dismiss THE MAN FROM U.N.C.L.E. as another rip-off of Ian Fleming, another fly-by-night copy riding the wave of James Bond's worldwide success. But the truth of the matter was somewhat different: Ian Fleming himself actually had a small hand in the development of the series.

To get the straight scoop on the genesis of THE MAN FROM U.N.C.L.E., it is necessary to go back to 1962, when television producer Norman Felton (known for producing such classic TV dramas as STUDIO ONE, DR. KILDARE and THE ELEVENTH HOUR) began to turn a critical eye on the programming his children watched on the tube. Although television was teeming with heroes— cops, cowboys and the like— Felton couldn't help but notice that all these characters were tall, dashing and tough, prone to win through the concept of "might-makes-right" rather than through any mental prowess. Why couldn't a TV hero be a smaller fellow who uses his brain to get himself out of a fix?

THE FLEMING CONNECTION

An opportunity to address this question soon arose when, in October 1962, the Ashley-Famous Agency brought Felton together with members of the prestigious J. Walter Thompson advertising firm. The Thompson group was considering the development of a series based on Ian Fleming's travel book THRILLING CITIES. An amusing but fairly plotless tour of major world cities, THRILLING CITIES seems an unlikely basis for a dramatic series, but the name Ian Fleming was hot in the wake of DR. NO, and any property bearing that name seemed a sure money-making opportunity.

After reading the book in galley form, Felton offered his prognosis: there was no series potential whatsoever to be found in the book. But he did have a few ideas of his own. . . Completely off the top of his head, Felton created a vivid portrait of a clever and sophisticated international hero, who he invited the executives to imagine was sitting in an adjoining room. Thompson executive Jack Ball saw some potential in this as-yet-unnamed character, and made arrangements for Felton to meet with Ian Fleming and discuss the concept.

Felton traveled to New York City to meet the internationally famous author of the Bond novels. The two men hit it off fairly well and enjoyed taking in the sights of the Big Apple. But Fleming, who was in poor health, seemed distracted, more interested in playing tourist than in working on a television concept. Towards the end of their New York visit, Felton began tossing out ideas for the character. Fleming provided a name: Solo. Fleming handed Felton some notes on Solo before they parted company, but these notes were quite sketchy. Felton was going to have to do most of the actual work himself.

Matters became complicated when the producers of the James Bond films, Harry Saltzman and Albert "Cubby" Broccoli, got wind of the SOLO project (SOLO being the working title of the embryonic series at this point) and urged Ian Fleming to disassociate himself from Felton's plans. Fleming bowed out graciously, and sold all his rights to Solo character, and the character name April Dancer, to Felton for one pound— about two dollars and fifty cents in American currency. NBC, the network with an eye on the Solo project, was disappointed to see Fleming go, but were still interested, and were not above mentioning Fleming's name in connection with the project in their promotional materials.

GIVING U.N.C.L.E. FORM AND FACE

Felton, meanwhile, still had a fairly sketchy concept on his hands, one which barely resembled the U.N.C.L.E. we've all come to know. Felton's Napoleon Solo seems to have been more of an independent operative (as his name obviously indicates) with sufficient personal resources to combat evil on his own, rather than an operative of a massive international law enforcement agency. But all of this was to change when Felton, fully aware that his notes were a weak foundation for a television series, gave those notes to Sam Rolfe, a writer and producer who had worked on the hit series HAVE GUN, WILL TRAVEL (as had future STAR TREK creator Gene Roddenberry).

Rolfe went back to square one, worked up a completely new and highly detailed background for Napoleon Solo (right down to the name of the person who cleans his apart-

ment!), and created the organization Napoleon would work for: the United Network Command for Law and Enforcement, better known simply as U.N.C.L.E. He also created some supporting characters: the Russian agent Illya Kuryakin (a brilliant brainstorm in an era when Russians were usually the villains in spy fiction) and the head of U.N.C.L.E., Mr. Allison.

Rolfe created a detailed organizational structure for U.N.C.L.E., and proposed a number of plots which would later wind up as actual episodes. [See the series premise chapter for "SOLO"] Despite all this work, Rolfe did not receive creator credit for the series.

MGM-Arena's original motivation for doing the series was simple: they wanted to play up the tenuous connection with Ian Fleming, and did everything in their power to suggest to the public that Fleming had created SOLO. (This would eventually lead to legal problems between Rolfe and Arena.) Rolfe's credit did not change after Fleming's lawyers insisted that MGM stop using Fleming's name in their publicity— Rolfe was still listed as a "developer." Early in 1964, when the pilot of SOLO was already in the can, another bombshell dropped: the producers of the Bond films requested that the name Solo be changed to something else.

Fleming had used a character called Solo in his novel GOLDFINGER, and the character was slated to appear in the upcoming movie version. They also charged that the whole idea of the show was a shameless Bond rip-off. The question came to court, but MGM-Arena got a much-needed edge when they produced a statement, signed by Ian Fleming himself, in which the Bond author (who had viewed the pilot) expressed his belief that SOLO did not infringe on his Bond series in any fashion.

The only concession gained by the Bond producers was a change in the name of the series: instead of being known by the contested SOLO title, it would now be called THE MAN FROM U.N.C.L.E. Ian Fleming died later that same year.

MEET MR. FLEMING

In an interview published in PARADE magazine for March 17, 1968, Norman Felton discussed U.N.C.L.E. in the wake of its cancellation and recalled how his reading of THRILLING CITIES led to the meeting with Ian Fleming in 1962.

"I read it," he recalls, "and flew to New York and London for meetings with Fleming, but he didn't come up with anything, except to say that he liked an idea I had about a small, witty, charming, intelligent international agent. In fact, he named the agent Napoleon Solo, and that was his sole contribution. He explained that he was too busy to work on the program and gave me a letter of release.

"Later when we finished the pilot, I called the program SOLO, but Fleming had used that last name in previous works, and the producers who had bought the rights to his books complained, so I changed the title to THE MAN FROM U.N.C.L.E. Actually I don't think the title meant very much to the show's success. The characters made it a success. McCallum and Vaughn were not cut in the pattern of the typical all-American hero. They were small, intelligent, unique, not particularly muscular, and the fans seemed to go for heroes of all nationalities. That's why the show was so successful both here and overseas. We offered a new type of hero."

CASTING CALL

Robert Vaughn, an up and coming actor, was not the first choice for the role of Napoleon Solo. By late September 1963, the casting department of Arena Productions sent Norman Felton a list of 41 names, to which he added another 6. None of the names on that list was Robert Vaughn's.

Actors on that original list included Rip Torn (who later guest-starred in the second season episode "The Alexander the Greater Affair") and Tony Franciosa. Other actors were J.D. Cannon, Peter Baldwin, Barry Nelson (who later appeared in "The Seven Wonders of the World Affair"), Robert Loggia (who soon starred in his own, albeit short-lived, series T.H.E. CAT), Jack Lord and Tom Tryon. Jack Lord may well have been eliminated for the same reason he was turned down when approach to play Capt. Kirk on STAR TREK—he wanted a large ownership percentage of the series he was starring in.

Other actors who were considered, but who didn't make the cut for one reason or another, included Michael Rennie, Darren McGavin, Robert Culp, Donald Harron, Jeremy Slate and William Shatner, all of whom eventually appeared on episodes of U.N.C.L.E. The list also included Lee Marvin, Lloyd Bridges, James Coburn, John Forsythe, Peter Graves, Leslie Nielsen, George Segal, Cliff Robertson, Christopher Plummer and Robert Redford. Some actors turned down the offer, preferring to pursue a motion picture career, while others were eliminated by the producers. Ultimately they chose a young actor named Robert Vaughn, who was then appearing on a just-canceled series named THE LIEUTENANT.

Robert Vaughn was 31 when he was cast in the role of the suave superspy and man of the world Napoleon Solo.

ADDITIONAL TALENT

David McCallum had not achieved as much notice in his career up to this point, having just completed the role of Judas in THE GREATEST STORY EVER TOLD before landing the small supporting role in the pilot for U.N.C.L.E.

The U.N.C.L.E. theme was written by Jerry Goldsmith, who also did the score for the pilot episode. Goldsmith did a lot of TV music in the sixties, including for such shows as

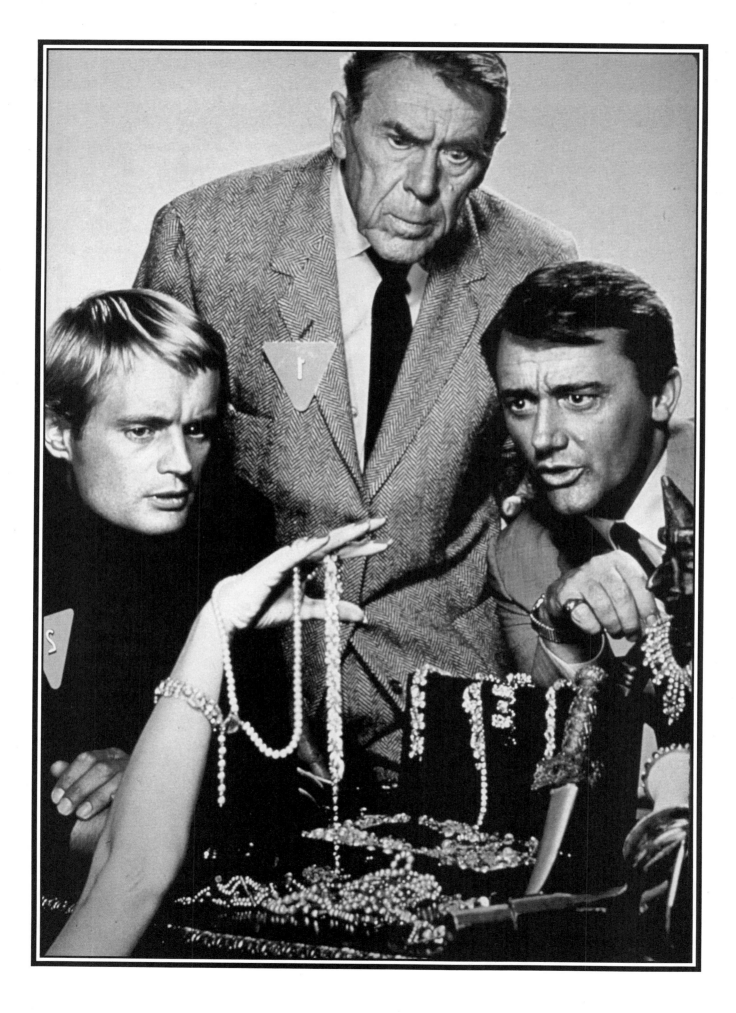

GUNSMOKE. In the 70's he began doing scores for major motion pictures and by the 80's was one of the most sought after film composers in Hollywood. His television theme work in the 60's definitely displays his talents. Unlike the all too often subdued music crafted for television shows today, Goldsmith's music was very brassy and stylistic.

His '60s U.N.C.L.E. music, heard nearly 30 years later, comes across as more modern sounding than much of what is done for television today. That's because the style of motion picture scores done today are in the classic, bravura style composers used on motion pictures decades ago and which was much in evidence on television in the '60s.

Cinematography on THE MAN FROM U.N.C.L.E. was often by Joseph Biroc and Fred Koenekamp, who both graduated to motion pictures such as the 1974 epic THE TOWERING INFERNO. Koenekamp also photographed the 1968 film SOL MADRID, which starred David McCallum, as well as PAPILLION (1973), DOC SAVAGE (1975) and THE CHAMP (1979).

THE PILOT EPISODE

The pilot for SOLO was filmed at a cost of $268,933 and was lensed in color. While the series was always planned to be in black and white (which it was during the first season) the pilot, as well as "The Double Affair," were shot in color. This is because MGM was already planning on releasing theatrical versions of some of the episodes in Europe. TO TRAP A SPY and THE SPY WITH MY FACE were the first two U.N.C.L.E. features. They both used the basic episodes with additional footage shot for the theatrical release. To save the trouble caused by needing to film additional scenes for the features, subsequent U.N.C.L.E. movies were based on two-part episodes which merely needed to be edited together to attain a feature length. A total of eight U.N.C.L.E. features were released although only the first three played theaters in the United States.

Unlike the average TV pilot which is filmed in a week, three weeks were spent by director Don Medford on "The Vulcan Affair" (TO TRAP A SPY) in order to achieve the feature length needed for the planned theatrical release.

Initially the pilot called THRUSH "Wasp" because MGM didn't think THRUSH sounded menacing enough. But when the show went to series, every mention of "Wasp" was redubbed in "The Vulcan Affair" with the word THRUSH and it has been that way ever since. When it was picked up as a series, the title was changed from SOLO to THE MAN FROM U.N.C.L.E. and the first regular series episode, "The Iowa Scuba Affair," went into production in May 1964 for a September airing.

THE U.N.C.L.E. PILOT

The pilot, originally entitled "The Vulcan Files," was changed to "The Vulcan Affair"— and every episode from that point on would be an "Affair" of one sort or another, perhaps because of the mild double entendre in the word "affair," lacking somewhat in the more prosaic "file." The first draft teleplay, by Sam Rolfe, was completed in November 1963.

"The Vulcan Affair" begins with the teaser which would be used in the first seven episodes. Illya and Napoleon Solo drive up to the brownstone storefront of Del Floria's tailor shop, as the narrator explains the basics. They walk into the shop and head for the back, walking past Del Floria as he steam-presses some garment or another, right up to the back of the store, through a fitting room, which opens and admits them to the U.N.C.L.E. reception area. They walk down corridors and pass other U.N.C.L.E. agents, armed and wearing badges like the ones Napoleon and Illya have donned. They reach the communications room, where Mr. Waverly is waiting. Illya assembles his special U.N.C.L.E.-issue gun, and Solo turns on one of the computers. Then he speaks directly to the camera:

"My name is Napoleon Solo. I'm an enforcement agent in section two here. . . that's operations and enforcement."

Illya, in turn, speaks:

"I am Illya Kuryakin. Also an enforcement agent. Like my friend Napoleon, I go and I do. . . whatever I am told by my chief."

Waverly, who has been fairly distracted up to this point, speaks last.

"Oh yes. . . Alexander Waverly, Number One, Section One. In charge of this, our New York headquarters. It's from here that I send these young men on their various missions."

The camera pulls back to a medium shot of these three characters, and the title of the episode is superimposed. "The Vulcan Affair" set the precedent for all future titles: all U.N.C.L.E. adventures would be called "affairs." "Files" had been considered, but "affair" was deemed a good deal more glamorous a term, with its slight sexual connotation and its suggestion of intrigue of all sorts.

INSIDE U.N.C.L.E.

The story proper begins with a raid on U.N.C.L.E.'s New York headquarters by agents of THRUSH. We first encounter the secret entrance through the fitting room in the back of Del Floria's Tailor Shop, and discover the nature of the U.N.C.L.E. security cards. We first see Napoleon Solo as the attackers fire on him. He is standing behind bulletproof glass, which cracks but does not yield to the hail of bullets. Solo shoots one of the attackers but the other enemy agents commit suicide with poison when they discover that they are trapped.

Differences between the original filmed pilot and the later series abound: Illya Kuryakin, played by David McCallum, is a minor supporting character here, and the head of U.N.C.L.E., was portrayed by Leo G. Carroll in the series, but in the theatrical ver-

sion of the pilot (which is the way it was originally filmed) actor Will Kuluva plays the head of U.N.C.L.E., Mr. Allison. THRUSH is known as WASP in the theatrical version as well. But Kuluva's scenes were cut and reshot by the time the series aired, although they are retained in TO TRAP A SPY.

A note on Section Two. Sam Rolfe actually sketched out an organizational plan for U.N.C.L.E., which looked something like this:

Section One: Policy and Operations

Section Two: Operations and Enforcement

Section Three: Enforcement and Intelligence

Section Four: Intelligence and Communications

Section Five: Communications and Security

Section Six: Security and Personnel

Section Seven: Propaganda and Finance

Section Eight: Camouflage and Deception

Note the overlap between various sections, especially the first two. Waverly was probably involved in both sections, since he was (as far as we know) the head of U.N.C.L.E.. The mysterious Mr. Allison?

Who knows. Suffice it to say, Waverly was in charge when the series began with the first THRUSH raid on U.N.C.L.E. in "The Vulcan Affair."

THE SECRETS OF U.N.C.L.E.

The assault on U.N.C.L.E. headquarters is action packed: THRUSH knows the way in and fakes the proper badges, but they don't know about the chemical in the real U.N.C.L.E. badges, and are detected. Unable to fight their way out, the THRUSH agents commit suicide with poison capsules.

The villain of the piece is Andrew Vulcan, head of United Global Chemicals— the East Coast front for THRUSH! The attempt to kill Waverly was the result of Waverly's discovery that Vulcan has arranged the assassination of the premier of Natumba, Ashumen. Napoleon Solo must get close to Vulcan. He does so through Elaine Bender, an old girlfriend of the evil executive. Solo and Elaine attend a party at Vulcan's place, but Vulcan spots Napoleon as an U.N.C.L.E. agent and sabotages his car.

Solo escapes, only to face an unusual plot twist when he and Elaine are captured by the premiere they are trying to save! Ashumen, a THRUSH agent, is behind the assassination plot— the real victims are to be his two top-ranking ministers. Through some tricky maneuvering, Napoleon manages to save himself, Elaine and the ministers, leaving Ashumen and Vulcan to their much-deserved fates: death in an explosion.

THE U.N.C.L.E. WAY

In recruiting Elaine Bender, the former college chum of Andrew Vulcan whom they arrange to have "accidentally" become reaquainted with Vulcan at a party, Solo explains that Vulcan is associated with THRUSH and describes THRUSH in the following manner.

"THRUSH might be a man. Or a woman. Or a committee of some sort. THRUSH is the head of a secret international organization. Very powerful, very wealthy. THRUSH has no allegiance to any country nor to any ideal. It will embark upon any undertaking which THRUSH may decide is in its own interest." Later that was altered so that THRUSH was the name of the organization itself, not of a person who headed it. In the television series THRUSH was never an acronym like U.N.C.L.E. although many U.N.C.L.E. fans know what THRUSH stands for. This is because in one of the Ace U.N.C.L.E. novels written by David McDaniel, that author decided that THRUSH was an acronym for Technological Hierarchy for the Removal of Undesirables and the Subjugation of Humanity. It was clearly in the tradition of Bond's old nemesis SPECTRE.

Although this meaning for THRUSH was never revealed on the television series itself, MGM approved all material used in the U.N.C.L.E. novels and was quick to reject anything which conflicted with material in the TV series. By approving McDaniel's definition for THRUSH, they allowed it to become part of the official canon by default.

And so, on Tuesday September 22, 1964, audiences witnessed the first enthralling episode of THE MAN FROM U.N.C.L.E., a TV series which would arguably be as popular in its time as James Bond was and which may yet make a comeback to rival agent 007.

Following is the original text of the 1964 promotional booklet for THE MAN FROM U.N.C.L.E. This is the premise provided NBC after the pilot episode, "The Vulcan Affair," had been filmed. The original style of the pamphlet, including the use of "all caps," has been retained as much as possible, although blatant spelling errors have been changed to avoid unnecessary confusion.

Chapter Two
"SOLO"

A NEW FULL-HOUR ADVENTURE SERIES

Produced by Arena Productions, Inc.
with MGM for the National Broadcasting Company.
METRO-GOLDWYN-MAYER TELEVISION
Presents
Arena Productions
New Full House Adventure Series
"SOLO"
Starring
ROBERT VAUGHN
as "Solo"
Also Starring
WILL KULUVA
as "Mr. Allison"
and
Co-starring
DAVID McCALLUM
as "Illya"
Executive Producer: Norman Felton
Developed by: Norman Felton and
Sam Rolfe

***

A Metro-Goldwyn-Mayer Television Presentation
in Association with the National Broadcasting Company

Produced by Arena Productions, Inc.

INTRODUCTION

"SOLO" IS FOR THOSE WHO DREAM OF HIGH ADVENTURE. INTERNATIONAL INTRIGUE. . . . SPINE-TINGLING DANGER. . . . ROMANTIC GLAMOUR. . . . THE BIZARRE. . . . THE BREATH-TAKING. . . THESE ARE THE THRILLS OF DREAMERS. . . . DAY-DREAMERS. . . . NIGHT DREAMERS. . . . . .

THIS FULL-HOUR SERIES TELLS THE EXCITING EXPLOITS OF NAPOLEON SOLO, SOPHISTICATED AGENT FOR U.N.C.L.E., A MYSTERIOUS ORGANIZATION DEDICATED TO COMBATING WORLD-WIDE CRIME AND THREATS TO THE WELFARE OF PEOPLE IN ANY COUNTRY ON THE GLOBE.

THIS IS "SOLO"

####

THE HIGH ROAD TO ADVENTURE—-

A suave but serious young man unexpectedly approaches and asks you to risk your life——

He is Napoleon Solo, an enforcement agent for U.N.C.L.E. This secret organization, headquartered in New York, faces problems of enormous scope. It battles international crime or anything which may affect large masses of people or nations or a dangerous local situation somewhere. . . anywhere.

Its principal enemy is Thrush, ruthless, powerful, evil world-wide group for hire.

Uncle may have to stop Thrush from firing a deadly missile from the United States into friendly Canada. . . Or find a "lost" tube of germ bacilli which can destroy millions. . . Or to discover why pet dogs in several cities have been trained to kill their masters.

U.N.C.L.E. will fight a deposed king who is using terrifying tear gas to become the emperor of the underworld. . . Or discover why the tractor ordered by a Siberian farmer turns out to be a walking, mechanical monster. . . Or to connect a strange packet of birdseed with a Central American revolution.

Solo explains that these crises, although bizarre, are very real. And that he always needs the help of ordinary, every-day people on his danger-filled missions. Thus these average citizens are suddenly swept away from their humdrum lives into a glorious moment. . . . . . . It could be you.

THIS IS U.N.C.L.E.

There is a row of buildings in New York City in the Fifties. It includes a Public Parking Garage, four dilapidated brownstone buildings and a fairly new, three-storied whitestone.

The first and second floors of the whitestone are taken up by an exclusive "key-club" restaurant named "The Mask Club". The third floor is a sedate suite of offices, the entrance to which bears the engraved letters "U.N.C.L.E." which gives the general appearance of a normal organization engaged in a special charity project or a Fund Foundation Headquarters. If one were to investigate he might learn that all these buildings are owned by U.N.C.L.E. and all the people involved are in its employ.

Behind these walls is one large building consisting of three floors of a modern complex office building. . . a maze of corridors and suites containing brisk, alert young personnel of many races, creeds, colors and national origins. . . as well as complex masses of modern machinery for business and communications.

Below basement level you would find that an underground channel has been cut through from the East River where several cruisers are anchored. If one could ascend to the roof and examine the large neon-lighted, advertising billboard there, a trained eye would see that its supporting pillars conceal a high powered short-wave antenna, as well as elaborate electronic receiving and sending gear.

This is the heart, brain and body of the organization named U.N.C.L.E. The initials have nothing to do with the United Nations. It's merely a code, called "Uncle" by the employees.

U.N.C.L.E. takes on anything that affects the welfare of people, or countries, or a dangerous local condition anywhere in the world. It can be international crime. . . political. . . bizarre!

AND THEN THERE IS THRUSH

There will be a recurrent series of encounters with an organization shaped somewhat like a darker convolution of U.N.C.L.E. This is an ingenious, well financed, highly scientific band of men and women working under the aegis of Thrush.

Thrush himself is an unknown cipher. Thrush might be a single man. . . or it might be a woman. . . . . . or it might even be a group.

Thrush is never seen, but its presence is always felt.

Thrush and its organization are, in the classic sense, the international group for hire. They may be used for one nation against another. Or where the profit is large enough Thrush may be in business for itself. Or where some special power may accrue to it, Thrush may enter the fray.

When Thrush is in the picture the opposition will be cunning, ruthless, and well-heeled in both cash and manpower.

THE MEN BEHIND THE CAMERA:

Norman Felton and Sam Rolfe, both award winners, are the co-developers of SOLO. Felton is executive producer and Rolfe wrote the initial teleplay. Both have had distinguished careers and professional experience which gives them ideal backgrounds for such a provocative adventure-suspense series.

THE EXECUTIVE PRODUCER   NORMAN FELTON

Norman Felton is executive producer of "Dr. Kildare", "The Eleventh Hour" and "The Lieutenant" for Metro-Goldwyn-Mayer

Television. He formerly was director of programs for CBS-TV on the west coast. During his years as producer-director, he received an Emmy Award for direction of "Robert Montgomery Presents", the TV Guide Gold Medal and the Look Magazine TV Award for the same series. He has also won two Sylvania Awards for distinguished achievement in creative television, two Christopher Awards and was the producer of "Studio One" when it was nominated for the Best Series Emmy. His other credits include "U.S. Steel Hour", "Goodyear Playhouse", "Alcoa Hour" and "Hallmark Playhouse".

DEVELOPER AND WRITER   SAM ROLFE

Sam Rolfe was producer of "The Eleventh Hour" during its entire first season as well as during the first shows for 1963-64. Earlier at CBS-TV, he was the co-creator and producer-writer of "Have Gun, Will Travel" and Produced "Hotel de Paree". In motion pictures, he was an Academy Award nominee for best original story and screenplay for "The Naked Spur", his first film assignment. He won the Box Office Champion Award for writing "The McConnell Story" with his other film credits including "Target Zero", "Pillars of the Sky" and "Bombers B-52".

NAPOLEON SOLO

Solo, an Enforcement Agent for U.N.C.L.E., is a dark, athletic-looking man with an easy-going manner and a quick smile. A bachelor, he often has been in love. He rather tends to view all men as equals unless their behavior proves them otherwise.

He is equally democratic in his attitude towards women. . . except where he adopts the Orwellian theorem in relation to the more attractive ones. . . . "except that some women are more equal than others. . . . . . "

Solo has a love for the sea. He owns a thirty foot sloop and when not sailing on the water, he is most likely in the water. He owns all the trappings of a scuba diver, also an expert on a surfboard. In winter, he gets a mild spell of ski fever.

Yet too much activity is offensive to his natural-born, off-duty streak of pure laziness. He can relax like few other mortals.

People who know Solo non-professionally believe that he is working for "one of those non-profit organizations, like a foundation. . . or something." They know that his job takes him out of town a lot, and "poor Solo must be accident-prone, judging by his appearance at times on his return." "Poor Solo" is quite the reverse of "accident prone." He is more than capable of taking care of himself. He always carries a weapon, an automatic pistol which gives devastating and compact fire power to a single man.

Solo isn't one of those "flip" characters although there is a soft humor prevalent when he is relaxed. Solo would tend to try to make people comfortable, which is, after all, only kindness.

He makes no high-blown moral statements about his work, nor his reasons for engaging in it. But he can only work for a "cause" that is in the right. . . and he takes satisfaction in the destruction of evil.

ROBERT VAUGHN. . . . . as. . . . . . . NAPOLEON SOLO

Robert Vaughn, the talented title star of "Solo", has appeared in some 300 top TV dramas and currently is a star of "The Lieutenant" series. His earlier television shows include "Playhouse 90", "The Eleventh Hour", "Dick Powell Show", "Twilight Zone", "Rawhide", "Rifleman" and many others. In motion pictures, he won an Academy nomination, the Laurel Award of the Motion Picture Exhibitor magazine and a Golden Globe nomination by the Hollywood Foreign Press Club for his performance in his second film, "The Young Philadelphians". He also co-starred in "The Magnificent Seven" and "The Caretakers". Following his start in west coast theatres, he made his film debut in "No Time To Be Young".

MR. ALLISON

Mr. Allison, a lean, dry, somewhat pedantic man, is Solo's boss, one of the top men with U.N.C.L.E. , currently serving as head of Policy and Operations Section One. Nothing exists in conversations with Mr. Allison except the purpose and job that is necessary to accomplish that purpose. His feelings run deeper than what appears but he does not hesitate to send agents off into terribly dangerous situations without sentimentality. If an agent is lost, the only question to be settled is, who will be sent to replace him.

WILL KULUVA. . . . . as. . . . . MR. ALLISON

Will Kuluva has had a versatile, distinguished career in television, motion pictures and on the Broadway stage. On TV he has appeared in "The Fugitive", "The Defenders", "Ben Casey", "Bonanza", "The Untouchables", "Alfred Hitchcock Presents", "Twilight Zone" and "Combat" among others. His films include "The Spiral Road", "Go Naked in the World", "Crime in the Streets", "The Shrike" and "Viva Zapata". On Broadway he played in "The Shrike", "Richard III", "My Three Angeles", "Doctor's Dilemma", "Hold On To Your Hats", "Darkness At Noon".

ADVENTURES IN THE FUTURE

Here are condensed examples of future stories planned for "Solo".

1. A dog turns into a four-footed weapon of terror, an attempt to kill a young corporation lawyer. Solo discovers that in various cities of the world animals have been trained to kill. The lap terrier turns on its master. The family Alsation becomes a stalking stranger. The stray mongrel you passed on the street might be the assassin who marked you for his victim. It's all part of an international plan to steal a multi-million dollar cartel through the use of a basic element. . . . . terror.

2. A deposed Middle Eastern King is forming an international empire of the underworld. His most powerful weapon is a new

nerve gas——a gas that sends the cat in flight from the mouse, the hawk in frenzied flight from the sparrow and turns men into terror-stricken hulks in slavish flight from everything. A New Jersey school teacher and Solo are pursued by two warring groups, and exposed to the gas.

3. A young, pretty girl, living on a Midwest farm, watches silos of wheat rising upward on the fields around her. One day she sees a silo going down. . . down into the ground. There's a missile in it. A band of international renegades try to take over that missile, re-direct it so it will fire onto the territory of a friendly nation. The farm girl was with Solo that night as he fought a stalking battle in a field of wheat against two men armed with rifles and infra-red sniper equipment. She was with him in Thrush's tunnel, and also in the silo near the finish.

4. Solo and a Florida house-wife are trudging through the quick-sand-laden, snake-infested traps of the Okefenokee Swamps, pur-sued by men from Thrush searching for them in their propeller dri-ven, monster-like swamp sleds, prepared to kill them on sight. It all started when a packet of strange-looking bird seed had been slipped into her grocery bag by a Seminole Indian boy behind the counter. Before she could return the bird-seed, intermixed with grayish metallic pellets which glowed in the dark, the men had come who had tried to murder her and Solo had arrived to protect her. Before it was over, she had learned what the packet of bird-seed would do to the Low Altitude-Detection System as well as the Shore-to Ship Radar System of the Florida coast, and of the vast international ram-ifications of Thrush's amazing plot.

5. A young couple honeymoon on a small freighter for the leisurely cruise down the coast of South America. Suddenly, near the Sargasso Sea, they are enveloped in a strange plot which results in the disap-pearance of ships from the face of the earth——and participate with Solo in his war against the mysterious "Q-Boats".

6. Terror finds a young American student and a French shop girl in the form of a plaque marking the spot where a "heroine" of the French resistance died in the uprising against the Occupation Forces in 1944. . . a "heroine" who was the mother of the girl. . . a "heroine" who comes back to life as the leader of a die-hard group of fanatics

bent on assassination, chaos and destruction. . . until Solo comes to fight them.

7. A Siberian farmer, a pioneer in the new area of the remote U.S.S.R., looks forward to only one forthcoming happy event—-the arrival of a new tractor. The tractor arrives, and as he proudly uncrates it, he discovers that he has received a walking, talking, mechanical monster designed for moon exploration. Thrush has deviated the shipment to his home for his own purpose. . . a purpose that almost succeeds until the arrival of Solo.

8. A middle-aged American sergeant, stationed in Japan, adopts an entire Japanese family as his own. When the adopted father is murdered, the sergeant, bent on revenge, goes on a search for the killers. . . and is precipitated into a situation involving an Imperial War Lord and a secret society. . . . . he also encounters Solo.

Pilot Episode: "The Vulcan Affair"

CAST

Starring

ROBERT VAUGHN. . . . . as. . . . . . . NAPOLEON SOLO

Also Starring

WILL KULUVA. . . . . as. . . . . . . MR. ALLISON

Guest Stars

PATRICIA CROWLEY. . . . . as. . . . . . . ELAINE MAY DONALD-SON

FRITZ WEAVER. . . . . . . as. . . . . . . VULCAN

WILLIAM MARSHALL. . . . . . . as. . . . . . . ASHUMEN

Co-Starring

IVAN DIXON. . . . . . . .as. . . . . . .SOUMARIN

DAVID McCALLUM. . . . . . . .as. . . . . . .ILLYA

With

Victoria Shaw. . . . . . . .as. . . . . . . .Gracie Ladovan
Rupert Crosse. . . . . . . .as. . . . . . . .Nobuk
Mario Siletti. . . . . . . .as. . . . . . . .Del Floria
and
Eric Berry. . . . . . . .as. . . . . . . .Alfred Ghist

Produced by NORMAN FELTON

Directed by DON MEDFORD

Developed and Written by SAM ROLFE

Production Associate JOSEPH GANTMAN

   Four men, bent on murder, slip stealthily into the camouflaged New York headquarters of U.N.C.L.E., secret organization to combat international crime and threats to the welfare of people in any country in the world. Their leader reaches the top level where Napoleon Solo, an enforcement agent, kills him.
   Mr. Allison, head of U.N.C.L.E. and the intended victim, gives Solo his assignment. Thrush, world-wide crime-for-hire syndicate, plans to take over Western Natumba, newly freed African nation, by assassinating its Premier Ashumen when he and his two aides visit the Vulcan Chemical plant.
   Solo enlists the help of Elaine May Donaldson one-time college sweetheart of Andrew Vulcan, an undercover Thrush officer. Following an intrigue-crammed evening at a formal Washington party given by Vulcan, Elaine goes with the tycoon on a night tour of his plant. There Vulcan explains an experimental reactor where a broken coupling would cause a massive explosion.

Solo, following, discovers this is how the murder is to be staged. Discovered, he is chased by guards and dogs through the plant. Elaine gets him out of the building and they find Ashumen to warn him. But the premier reveals he is with Thrush, that it is his two accompanying aides who are to die the next morning.

Solo and Elaine are suspended by chains to a water pipe in a locked underground tunnel. He eventually frees them and reaches the research room just as the fatal reactor is started.

THE GUEST STARS

PATRICIA CROWLEY. . . . . . . as. . . . . . . ELAINE MAY DONALD-SON

Patricia Crowley guest-stars as a house-wife thrust into the danger-ous international intrigue of "The Vulcan Affair", opening episode of "Solo". An extremely popular television and motion picture actress, she played the title role in TV's "A Date With Judy" for 39 weeks, has since appeared in "The Lieutenant", "The Eleventh Hour", "Dr. Kildare", "Alfred Hitchcock Presents", "Mr. Novak", "The Virginian", "Playhouse 90", "Climax", "Schlitz Playhouse", "Bonanza", "Kraft Mystery Theatre" and others. Her motion pic-tures include "The Wheeler Dealers", "There's Always Tomorrow", "Key Witness", "The Square Jungle", "Hollywood or Bust", "Money From Home" and "Forever Female".

FRITZ WEAVER. . . . . . . as. . . . . . . ANDREW VULCAN

A television and Broadway star, Fritz Weaver portrays Vulcan, head of an industrial empire and secret officer of Thrush, powerful world-wide crime syndicate in "The Vulcan Affair", initial show of "Solo". On television, Weaver has appeared in "Dr. Kildare", "The Defenders", "Playhouse 90", "Play of the Week", "U.S. Steel Hour" and "Studio One" among many. He twice played Shakespeare on television, as Brutus in "Julius Caesar" and in "She Stoops to Conquer" on "Omnibus". On Broadway, he won the Clarence Derwent Award for his performance in "The White Devil". He spent three seasons at the American Shakespeare Festival and recently made his motion picture debut in "Fail Safe".

WILLIAM MARSHALL. . . . . . . as. . . . . . . ASHUMEN

Internationally prominent screen and stage player, William Marshall portrays the Premier of Western Natumba, newly independent African nation, in "The Vulcan Affair", opening episode of "Solo". Marshall's American motion pictures are "Something of Value", "The Gladiators" and "Lydia Bailey". He recently completed the Spanish film, "Piedra de Toque". Marshall appeared on the London stage in "Toys in the Attic" and toured Europe and Great Britain in "Othello", produced by the Dublin Theatre Festival.

CO-STAR

IVAN DIXON. . . . . . . as. . . . . . . SOUMARIN

Ivan Dixon plays the Economics Minister of Western Natumba in "The Vulcan Affair", initial show of "Solo". Active in television, motion pictures and the Broadway stage, his many TV credits include "Dr. Kildare", "Perry Mason", "Studio One", "Twilight Zone", "Dick Powell Show", "Have Gun, Will Travel", "DuPont Show of the Month". He appeared in "Raisin in the Sun", both in the motion picture and on Broadway and has been in five other films and many New York plays.

THE DIRECTOR OF THE PILOT EPISODE
DON MEDFORD

Don Medford, winner of a Christopher Award, directed all "General Electric Theatre" shows for three years, produced and directed "The Corrupters", directed, among many others, "Dr. Kildare", "The Eleventh Hour", "Mr. Novak", "The Lieutenant", "Twilight Zone", "The Dick Powell Show", "Alfred Hitchcock Presents", "Climax", "Suspicion", "The Kraft Theatre", "Robert Taylor's Detectives", the "June Allyson Show" and "The Rifleman". Before entering television, he was a Broadway play producer.

NORMAN FELTON

Norman Felton, award-winning producer, director and writer and Director of Programs for Metro-Goldwyn-Mayer Television, is executive producer of "Solo", a new full-hour dramatic suspense series for the NBC Network.

He is also executive producer of three of MGM-TV's important series on NBC—-"Dr. Kildare" (in its third season), "The Eleventh Hour" (second season) and "The Lieutenant". Prior to joining MGM in 1960, Felton was with CBS-TV for four years as an executive producer and then as west coast director of programs for the network. During his years as a producer-director, he received the Emmy Award for direction of "Robert Montgomery Presents" and the Look Magazine TV Award and the TV Guide Gold Medal for the same series.

He has also won two Sylvania Awards for distinguished achievement in creative television, two Christopher Awards, and was the producer for "Studio One" when it was nominated for the Best Series Emmy.

A naturalized citizen, Felton was born in London, England. He left school at fourteen and came to the U.S., working first as a truck driver in Cleveland. He became interested in Little Theatres and began writing plays. He won the Rockefeller Playwriting Fellowship in 1938-9 and 1939-40. During the two years, he wrote plays and directed in civic theatres in the Midwest.

After publication of his award-winning plays "Rusty Gun" (Sergel Prize & St. Louis Award), and "Sam 'n' Ella" (National Playwriting Prize), he taught playwriting and experimental techniques at the University of Iowa.

His creative experimentation with development of new techniques of staging resulted in his joining NBC-Radio in 1943 to produce radio programs with "originality".

He remained a producer-director with NBC-Radio until 1948, doing such shows as "Author's Playhouse", "Grand Hotel", "First Nighter", "The Guiding Light" and others. His TV work began in 1948 when he became executive producer for NBC-TV in Chicago, assigned to build new dramatic and variety programs.

During this period as producer-director of "Crisis", "Stud's Place", and "Garroway at Large", "Felton came to the attention of Robert Montgomery who brought him to New York at the beginning of his new series, "Robert Montgomery Presents". This began a five-year association during which Felton wrote many originals and adaptations for the series and directed over one hundred of the plays. He also directed the "Goodyear Playhouse", "Alcoa Hour" and "Hallmark Playhouse".

Leaving Montgomery in 1955, he directed two seasons of "U.S. Steel Hour". In 1957-58, he was producer of "Studio One" in New York and Hollywood for CBS-TV, until he became an executive producer for the network in 1959. The following year, he was appointed west coast director of programs.

ROBERT VAUGHN

Robert Vaughn, one of Hollywood's most respected young actors, stars in the title role of MGM-TV's "Solo", full-hour dramatic suspense series for the NBC Network.

Vaughn currently is starring as Captain Rambridge opposite Gary Lockwood in MGM-TV's series, "The Lieutenant", a drama of the professional and personal lives of the peacetime Marines.

Vaughn, something of an "actor's actor", has, in the short span of his career, won such honors as an Academy Award nomination for "Best Supporting Actor", the Laurel Award of Motion Picture Exhibitor magazine and a Golden Globe nomination by the Hollywood Foreign Press Club.

He was born in New York City on November 30. His mother, Marcella Gaudel was a Broadway stage star; his father, Walter Vaughn, a famed radio actor.

Raised in Minneapolis, Minn., Vaughn entered the University of Minnesota School of Journalism, found himself migrating to the drama department where he starred in the University productions of "Hamlet", "Death Takes A Holiday" and "Knickerbocker Holiday".

It was while attending college in 1951 that he won the Phillip Morris Inter-Collegiate radio acting contest which caused him to give up a journalism career in favor of acting.

He entered Los Angeles City College in 1952 as a drama major where he starred in "Mr. Roberts". During his summer vacations he worked as resident director and leading man at Albuquerque, New Mexico, Summer Theatre in 1953-54.

Graduating with a BA in Drama in 1956, Vaughn earned his first paycheck as a professional actor in Los Angeles' Players' Ring production of "End As A Man". Impressed by the young actor's performance, Hecht-Hill-Lancaster signed him to a contract which proved to be short-lived.

Vaughn was called into the Army.

Following his days in uniform he signed with Columbia where he starred in "No Time To Be Young", next won a role in Warner Brothers' "The Young Philadelphians", for which he won his "Oscar" nomination.

He has since starred in more than 300 top TV dramas, including "Playhouse 90", "The Eleventh Hour", "Rawhide", "Dick Powell Show", "Twilight Zone" and others.

In films Vaughn co-starred with Yul Brynner in "The Magnificent Seven", and with Joan Crawford in "The Caretakers". In his spare time, Vaughn likes to return to the legitimate stage for a change of pace. He starred in the Los Angeles production of "Under the Yum Yum Tree" in 1962. He also is studying for his Doctor of Philosophy degree at the University of Southern California.

Chapter Three

A LEGACY OF SPIES

Once THE MAN FROM U.N.C.L.E. got off the ground, and a slow ratings period was surpassed, the series became a hit. The critics bashed it, of course (particularly Cleveland Amory), since they were probably already tired of this particular trend in popular entertainment, and justifiably annoyed by MGM's early efforts to link the series with Ian Fleming. The series premiered on Tuesday nights at 8:30 (hour-long shows often began at odd times during this period, unlike today), but stiff competition forced a move to Tuesdays in January, 1965. Then the series was able to achieve greater ratings— never mind the critics—the public ate it up like a fantastic new candy.

It took a while for the character of Illya Kuryakin to come into his own, as no one had worked up a detailed backstory for the character portrayed by David McCallum. Perhaps the mystery of the character added to his growing popularity, for he soon began to feature in the stories to a greater degree, eventually sharing equal billing with Robert Vaughn.

Even so, very little was ever revealed about Illya. We do know that he was single (despite the fact that McCallum, who was married to actress Jill Ireland at the time, did not remove his wedding ring while shooting the series). He was also still a Soviet citizen, not a defector, and U.N.C.L.E. is, after all, an international organization that is supposedly above politics. In one episode we learn that Illya is still an officer in the Soviet Navy.

But there was a reason for the shroud of mystery which continued to hang over Illya. That's the way David McCallum wanted it.

"Throughout U.N.C.L.E. my attitude was to play Kuryakin as a complete enigma. Everybody used to say they knew all about him, but there were no facts on record whatsoever in any show on who he was, where he came from or what his background was, except that he was born in Russia. So without specifying it, it established a slight mystery.

That was my choice, you know. I used to go through the scripts and eliminate anything about him. I remember in one script, someone asked me if I was married and I was supposed to say that I had been a long time ago. But I changed the line to some quote from Byron or Shelley like, 'Had I but time and tide. . .' "

THE STYLE OF U.N.C.L.E.

The show had to frequently take into account the age and poor health of the actor who played Mr. Waverly, Leo G. Carroll. Carroll was in his early seventies when he signed on with THE MAN FROM U.N.C.L.E., and could only work a few hours a day due to fatigue and poor concentration. His scenes were usually shot first thing each morning, so he could take the rest of the day off. Carroll was a real trouper, though, and stayed with the series to the bitter end, adding an element of class and humor throughout its run.

The first episode after the premiere was "The Iowa-Scuba Affair," helmed by future Superman director Richard Donner. Featuring film veteran Slim Pickens as the heavy, and Katherine Crawford as Jill

Dennison, this was an affair packed with wit and paradox. An attempt on Napoleon Solo's life is foiled, and his assailant, a soldier, is killed.

The discovery of scuba gear concealed in the dead man's motorcycle— in Iowa, miles from any water— leads to an investigation. It seems that the dead man's girlfriend, Jill Dennison, lives near a secret air base, and her neighbor, Cliff Spinner (Pickens), is digging a well on his property. It all looks pretty suspicious, especially after the discovery of a new plane on the base: Spinner is after it and its nuclear weaponry, but Napoleon perseveres and foils his plans. THRUSH was nowhere to be found in this outing. The heavy was just a farmer trying to cash out by helping a would-be Latin American dictator get his hands on some advance weaponry.

Beyond the THRUSH organization itself, THE MAN FROM U.N.C.L.E. rarely featured recurring adversaries. While WILD WILD WEST's Jim West had Miguelito Loveless and Maxwell Smart of GET SMART had Siegfried— Napoleon and Illya rarely faced the same villain twice. When they did, it was always a villainess. The third U.N.C.L.E. adventure, "The Quadripartite

Affair," featured Gervaise Ravel (Anne Francis), the only villainess to return and be played by the same actress.

After Yugoslavian scientist Professor Raven is killed, his daughter Marion seeks the aid of U.N.C.L.E. (Marion was portrayed by Jill Ireland, who was married to David McCallum at the time— she would return as Marion in the sequel, as well in another role further down the line.) When Solo and Illya investigate, the trail leads them to the yacht of Gervaise Ravel. A package of candy sent to Marion releases a gas which induces a paralyzing fear in its victim, Illya. Solo discovers Illya in this state— and Marion is missing. He finds her a prisoner on Gervaise's yacht and they escape.

Marion and our heroes head to Yugoslavia to track down the creator of the fear gas, one Karadian, only to have their plane blown out of the sky by a missile! Fortunately, the plane was really a remote-controlled drone; they were actually on a helicopter. The action soon centers on a concealed mountain hideaway, which blows up once the good guys have made their final escape. Good news: Marion and Illya have hit it off. Bad news: Gervaise Ravel has

escaped as well, leaving the way open for a sequel.

POPULAR VILLAINS

It didn't take long, either. The seventh U.N.C.L.E. episode was "The Giuoco Piano Affair," whose title referred to a chess move. And a chess game occurs as a backdrop in this affair: producers Norman Felton, Sam Rolfe and Joseph Calvelli all play or kibbitz, as does episode director Richard Donner as a drunkard.

Word reaches U.N.C.L.E. that Gervaise Ravel and her lover/accomplice Harold Bufferton are holed up in a small Peruvian town. When the agent who discovered them is killed, Waverly sends in Solo, and Illya talks the reluctant Marion Raven into acting as the bait in this deadly game. Marion has flourished in America, and is throwing a hip party, from which Illya basically drags her away. Down in Peru, a fiesta is underway, providing a colorful background to this tale. After Illya foils an attempt to capture Marion, Napoleon puts a bug on her, and she is abducted successfully the next time. Bufferton finds the device and destroys it, but there is another bug on

Marion, surgically implanted under the skin of her arm.

Napoleon and the local police surround Gervaise's yacht, but the villainess manages to escape, with Marion still in her clutches. The raid reveals the second bug, and Gervaise gets a doctor to remove it from Marion. A local cop bought out by Gervaise makes matters tough for Solo, but Solo escapes and the yacht blows up. Illya tracks Marion to a cabin but must kill Bufferton to free her.

Gervaise vows revenge and sets her Indian minions to capture our heroes. The corrupt official gain troubles Napoleon, and Gervaise seems to have won at last, but the local authorities, alerted by Solo, show up and save the day. When everyone returns to New York, Marion is surprised to find that her party is still going at full strength, even though she's been gone four days. She throws Solo out. As far as she's concerned, he's a bad influence on Illya.

SECOND SEASON

The other master criminal to plague U.N.C.L.E. more than once was the mysterious Dr. Egret, a female master of disguise who was planned as a recurring character but who only appeared twice. Her changing appearance was a handy ploy to avoid needing the same actress more than once! The first Dr. Egret was played by future BATMAN Catwoman Lee Meriwether in the first season's "The Mad, Mad Tea Party Affair." Her second outing was largely in another guise in "The Girls of Nazarone Affair" later that season; there she was played by Marion Moses.

The second season just happened to be the year that NBC went to full-scale color broadcasting. This, of course, meant that from now on, THE MAN FROM U.N.C.L.E. would be shot in color as well.

Producer Sam Rolfe moved on to other projects and was replaced by David Victor, whose credits included work on Norman Felton's DR. KILDARE series a few years earlier. Felton and Victor pretty much saw eye to eye on the direction the show was to take: it would stay the same. It was a winner— why mess with it? With the various imitators of the show getting wilder and wackier at every turn, there was no need to strive for more humor or mass appeal. U.N.C.L.E. worked well enough just as it was.

SINCERE FLATTERY

It might be a bit of a stretch to say that I, SPY was a rip-off of U.N.C.L.E. It was actually a very good show, with a brand of humor that sprang more from the interplay between Robert Culp and Bill Cosby (the first black actor in a lead series role) than from anything else, with stories that were a good deal more dramatic most of the time. But THE WILD WILD WEST was obviously a high concept show. You can almost imagine someone pitching it as "THE MAN FROM U.N.C.L.E. set in the late Nineteenth Century Old West."

It owed a lot to the U.N.C.L.E. formula. But if any one series ever owed its life to THE MAN FROM U.N.C.L.E., it was that ultimate parody of spy mania, GET SMART. The phone-booth opening was obviously inspired by Napoleon and Ilya's weekly trek through Del Floria's tailor shop. THE MAN FROM U.N.C.L.E.'s influence can be seen in a show as recent as SCARECROW AND MRS. KING, in which the U.N.C.L.E. conceit of the innocent young middle-class woman being drawn into espionage was repeated every week, but with the same woman every time, in this case Kate Jackson. Obviously,

Norman Felton was on to something way back in the early sixties.

GUEST STARS

A few ideas for the second season never quite came off. Victor would have liked to have had Liberace and the Beatles on the show (in the same episode? Probably not), but it never came to pass. Even so, THE MAN FROM U.N.C.L.E. was enough of a success to attract name actors instead of casting call veterans. (See "The Guests Of U.N.C.L.E.")

Later in the season, David Victor was promoted within Arena Productions, and Mort Abrams took over. The last two episodes of the season were produced by Douglas Benton, who would go on to produce the series spin-off, THE GIRL FROM U.N.C.L.E., the next year.

The second season kicked off with the first two-parter for the series, "The Alexander The Greater Affair." This story, which starred Rip Torn and Dorothy Provine, was also made into a theatrical feature. (See "U.N.C.L.E. At The Movies.") Season highlights included Vincent Price in "The Fox And Hounds Affair" and

"The Bat Cave Affair," which starred Martin Landau as a vampirish count.

But if THE MAN FROM U.N.C.L.E. had some serious impact on other television shows of the time, it was about to face a show that would impact on it, seriously challenge (and steal) its ratings, and force U.N.C.L.E.'s producers to the unwise maneuver of adding camp to their stories. That series was the biggest overnight sensation of the decade: BATMAN.

THIRD SEASON

Like that other venerable series, STAR TREK, THE MAN FROM U.N.C.L.E.'s third season is widely regarded as its worst. But while STAR TREK had some fairly good episodes mixed in with the bad, THE MAN FROM U.N.C.L.E.'s third year was truly awful. The reason: camp. It worked for BATMAN, which provided the first blow to U.N.C.L.E.'s dominance of the hip new color airwaves ratings. Why shouldn't it work for Illya and Napoleon?

It was just too silly. BATMAN may have worked as camp due primarily to the inherent absurdity of crime fighters in tights, but the heavy-handed attempt to crash in on that fad merely served to override the natural wit that could be found in any good U.N.C.L.E. story idea. The jokes might have been tolerable if THE MAN FROM U.N.C.L.E. hadn't run into a veritable desert in its third year, a drought-stricken area where few good scripts were to be found. Napoleon Solo's lechery became more pronounced, perhaps in an attempt to sex up the scripts, but all this did was make the hero look like an idiot who'd lost all sense of proportion.

The same problem plagued THE GIRL FROM U.N.C.L.E., which didn't even last a full season. THE MAN FROM U.N.C.L.E. was given one more chance. Boris Ingster and producer Irving Pearlberg were removed and replaced by producer Anthony Spinner, who had just departed from Quinn Martin's THE INVADERS. Norman Felton, no longer distracted by the short-lived GIRL FROM U.N.C.L.E. or his unrelated series JERICHO, also renewed his hands-on interest in THE MAN FROM U.N.C.L.E..

U.N.C.L.E.'S LAST STAND

THE MAN FROM U.N.C.L.E. backed off on the camp element in its fourth and final season, with the happy result that some of its scripts were more grounded in sensible dramatics. The newest producer for the show, Anthony Spinner, had very little time to get all this together, however, and some episodes were still fairly poor. The good ones did not sway NBC from their resolve to cancel the show in mid-season. Disappointed that their cash cow had gone dry, they gave U.N.C.L.E. the ax. It would be fifteen years before the thread of its world-wide mission was picked up once again.

Chapter Four

ROBERT VAUGHN IS NAPOLEON SOLO

Crazes come and crazes go and perhaps no medium is influenced by them quite so profoundly as television. When the release of GOLDFINGER in 1964 triggered a James Bond craze, television was quick to capitalize on the boom in spy stories. In fact, inspired by the success of the two earlier Bond films, DR. NO and FROM RUSSIA WITH LOVE, producer Norman Felton was already anticipating the forthcoming trend.

The co-creator of U.N.C.L.E., Norman Felton, had corresponded with Bond creator Ian Fleming who suggested some ideas that Felton later incorporated into his own plans. Fleming's contributions amounted to little more than some character names, but they were pure Fleming. It's easy to believe that a man who could conceive of the name Pussy Galore would also come up with the equally colorful (albeit less suggestive) name of April Dancer.

April Dancer, THE GIRL FROM U.N.C.L.E., would be introduced in an episode of THE MAN FROM U.N.C.L.E. and then spun off into her own series. But the other name Fleming suggested was Solo, who would march on screen as the title character in the pilot filmed for THE MAN FROM U.N.C.L.E., which would initially be titled SOLO when the concept was sold to NBC. What Fleming neglected to tell Felton was that Solo had been the name of a minor hood in the novel GOLDFINGER, which Felton had never read.

Norman Felton gave what he had to writer/producer Sam Rolfe to develop. Rolfe had worked on the popular western show HAVE GUN WILL TRAVEL about a dapper trouble-shooter who lived high when he wasn't on a mission or assignment of some sort. The character of Napoleon Solo as developed by Rolfe owed much to the glib persona of Palladin on that old western series.

THE TELEVISION CREDITS OF ROBERT VAUGHN

Series
THE LIEUTENANT (1963-64)
THE MAN FROM U.N.C.L.E. (1964-68)
THE PROTECTORS (1972-73)
EMERALD POINT N.A.S. (1983-84)
DANGER THEATER (1993 — Host)

Guest Appearances — Original air date
MEDIC: "Black Friday" (Nov. 21, 1955)
BIG TOWN: "Marine Story" (May 29, 1956)
GUNSMOKE: "Cooter" (May 19, 1956)
THE WEST POINT STORY: "The Operator and the Martinet"
(Oct. 12, 1956)
THE MILLIONAIRE: "The Story of Jay Powers" (Nov. 21, 1956)
ZANE GRAY THEATRE: "Courage is a Gun" (Dec. 14, 1956)
TELEPHONE TIME: "The Consort" (Jan. 27, 1957)
ZANE GRAY THEATRE: "A Gun is for Killing" (Oct. 18, 1957)
TALES OF WELLS FARGO: "Billy the Kid" (Oct. 21, 1957)
GUNSMOKE: "Romeo" (Nov. 9, 1957)
PLAYHOUSE 90: "The Trouble-Makers" (Nov. 21, 1957)
DRAGNET: "The Big Pack Rat" (May 1, 1958)
WAGON TRAIN: "The John Wilbot Story" (June 11, 1958)
JEFFERSON DRUM: "Return" (Oct. 30, 1958)
THE RIFLEMAN: "The Apprentice Sheriff" (Dec. 9, 1958)
BRONCO: "Borrowed Glory" (Feb. 24, 1959)
PLAYHOUSE 90: "Made In Japan" (March 5, 1959)
RIVERBOAT: "About Roger Mowbray" (Sept. 27, 1959)
THE LINEUP: "Prelude to Violence" (Nov. 4, 1959)
ALFRED HITCHCOCK PRESENTS: "Dry Run" (Nov. 8, 1959)
WICHITA TOWN: "Passage to the Enemy" (Dec. 2, 1959)
LAW OF THE PLAINSMAN: "The Dude" (Dec. 3, 1959)
"The Innocent" (Dec. 10, 1959)
ALCOA THEATRE: "The Last Flight Out" (Jan. 25, 1980)
THE REBEL: "Noblesse Oblige" (Feb. 14, 1960)
CHECKMATE: "Interrupted Honeymoon" (Sept. 24, 1960)
LARAMIE: "The Dark Trail" (Nov. 1, 1960)
THE JUNE ALLYSON SHOW: "Emergency" (Dec. 8, 1960)
WAGON TRAIN: "The Roger Bigelow Show" (Dec. 21, 1960)
THRILLER: "The Ordeal of Dr. Cordell" (March 7, 1961)
MALIBU RUN: "The Landslide Adventure" (May 10, 1961)
FOLLOW THE SUN: "A Rage for Justice" (Sept. 17, 1961)
TALES OF WELLS FARGO: "Treasure Coach" (Oct. 14, 1961)
TARGET! THE CORRUPTERS: "To Wear A Badge" (Dec. 1, 1961)
FOLLOW THE SUN: "The Far Side of Nowhere" (Dec. 17, 1961)
87th PRECINCT: "The Heckler" (Dec. 18, 1961)
CAIN'S HUNDRED: "The Debasers" (Jan. 16, 1962)
THE DICK POWELL SHOW: "The Boston Terrier" (April 10, 1962)
KRAFT MYSTERY THEATRE: "Death of a Dream" (June 20, 1962)
BONANZA: "The Way Station" (Oct. 29, 1962)
THE ELEVENTH HOUR: "The Blues My Baby Gave To Me"
(Dec. 12, 1962)
G.E. TRUE: "Defendant: Clarence Darrow" (Jan. 13, 1963)
EMPIRE: "No Small Wars" (Feb. 5, 1963)

THE VIRGINIAN: "If You Have Tears" (Feb. 13, 1963)
THE UNTOUCHABLES: "The Charlie Argos Story" (April 16, 1963)
77 SUNSET STRIP: "Your Fortune for a Penny" (May 31, 1963)
THE ELEVENTH HOUR: "The Silence of Good Men" (Oct. 9, 1963)
POLICE WOMAN: "Blast" (Jan. 24, 1975)
COLUMBO: "Troubled Waters" (Feb. 9, 1975)
POLICE WOMAN: "Generation of Evil" (Feb. 10, 1976)
COLUMBO: "Last Salute to the Commodore" (May 2, 1976)
CAPTAINS AND THE KINGS [mini-series]
(Sept. 30, 1976 to Nov. 25, 1976)
FEATHER AND FATHER: "The Golden Fleece" (June 11, 1977)
CENTENNIAL [mini-series] (Oct. 1, 1978 to Feb. 4, 1979)
THE GREATEST HEROES OF THE BIBLE: "The Story of Daniel and the
Lion" (Nov. 21, 1978)
HAWAII 5-0: "The Spirit is Willie" (Jan. 25, 1979)
BACKSTAIRS AT THE WHITE HOUSE [mini-series] (Jan. 29, 1979 to
Feb. 19, 1979)
TRAPPER JOHN, M.D.(Nov. 23, 1980)
THAT MAN IN THE WHITE HOUSE: FDR (1984)

Feature Films (* indicates an U.N.C.L.E. feature film)
NO TIME TO BE YOUNG (1957)
TEENAGE CAVE MAN (1958)
THE YOUNG PHILADELPHIANS (1959 — Received Oscar nomination)
GOOD DAY FOR A HANGING (1959)
THE MAGNIFICENT SEVEN (1960)
THE BIG SHOW (1961)
THE CARETAKERS (1963)
TO TRAP A SPY (1966)*
THE SPY WITH MY FACE (1966)*
ONE SPY TOO MANY (1966)*
ONE OF OUR SPIES IS MISSING (1966)*
THE VENETIAN AFFAIR (1967)
THE SPY IN THE GREEN HAT (1967)*
THE KARATE KILLERS (1967)*
BULLITT (1968)
THE HELICOPTER SPIES (1968)*
HOW TO STEAL THE WORLD (1968)*
THE BRIDGE AT REMAGEN (1969)
THE MIND OF MR. SOAMES (1970)
JULIUS CAESAR (1970)
THE STATUE (1971)
CLAY PIGEON (1971)
THE TOWERING INFERNO (1974)
BABYSITTER (1975)
DEMON SEED (1977)
STARSHIP INVASIONS (1977)
HANGAR 18 (1978)
BRASS TARGET (1978)
GOOD LUCK MISS WYCOTT (1979)
KEY WEST CROSSING (1979)
BATTLE BEYOND THE STARS (1980)
SUPERMAN III (1983)

But Palladin had been a loner, and while the name Napoleon Solo seemed to imply the same thing, he was anything but a lone agent. In the tradition of James Bond, Solo was a flashy espionage agent. But while Bond worked for the British Secret Service, Solo worked for an international organization based in New York. Perhaps inspired by SPECTRE in the Bond films, which began the tradition of secret, powerful organizations employing acronyms, Napoleon Solo worked for U.N.C.L.E., the United Network Command for Law Enforcement.

Initial press releases credit Fleming with creating the forthcoming series called SOLO, but the producers of the James Bond movies found out about this and threatened to sue MGM for stealing the name of a character from their soon to be released film GOLDFINGER. Fleming signed a sworn statement insisting that U.N.C.L.E. and James Bond were nothing alike, and the matter was dropped. But so was Fleming's name so far as having any connection with the U.N.C.L.E. series.

TURNING POINT

Born in New York City on November 2, 1932, Robert grew up in a family of performers. His father, Walter Vaughn, was an accomplished radio actor who was appearing on such popular shows as GANGBUSTERS. Vaughn's mother, Marcella Gaudel, was a leading lady on Broadway. Robert was largely raised by his grandparents in Minneapolis, where he grew up. When he went to college he chose the University of Minnesota School of Journalism. But when Robert won the Philip Morris Intercollegiate radio acting contest in 1951 he switched from the journalism department to drama and his career direction had been established.

In 1952 he transferred to Los Angeles City College. Because of the West Coast location of the school, he was able to work in theater during the summer vacations at the Albuquerque Summer Theatre. Following a short stint in the army, Vaughn graduated with a B.A. in drama. Vaughn then continued attending L.A. City College where he received a Master's degree and a Ph.D in political science.

His first professional acting work was on television in 1955 on such shows as MEDIC, GUNSMOKE, BIG TOWN, THE WEST POINT STORY and THE MILLIONAIRE. He continued doing episodic TV work in the late fifties even after he began landing film roles. Robert Vaughn's career extended into films in 1957 with NO TIME TO BE YOUNG.

An all but forgotten film role was the 1958 movie TEENAGE CAVE MAN, made when Vaughn was 25. This low budget science fiction film deals with Vaughn as a youth living and dealing with brutal humans in his tribe as well as dinosaurs (stock footage from the 1940 ONE MILLION B.C.). The "surprise" ending is when Vaughn finds a dying man wearing a protective suit who reveals that civilization was destroyed in an atomic war and that Vaughn and his people are the new hope of the human race. The film had remained obscure for many years until the Cinemax cable network revived it in 1991, along with other all but forgotten fifties science fiction films.

Within a year of making TEENAGE CAVE MAN, Vaughn had distinguished himself in the 1959 film THE YOUNG PHILADELPHIANS to such a degree that he was nominated for an Oscar for his performance. He landed another high profile film role in the now classic 1960 western THE MAGNIFICENT SEVEN.

THE ROAD TO U.N.C.L.E.

In 1963, Robert Vaughn was cast as the co-star of THE LIEUTENANT. While Gary Lockwood was the star, Vaughn had the pivotal role of Capt. Ray Rambridge. Set at the Camp Pendleton, California Marine base, Vaughn played Lockwood's commanding officer whose strictness and words of wisdom were all aimed at making Lt. William Rice (Lockwood) a better and more humane officer. Created and produced by Gene Roddenberry, he and Robert Vaughn's liberalism worked well together as the show often tried to use the Marine Corp setting to explore issues which were relevant to the time, such as racism.

It was while Vaughn was working on THE LIEUTENANT that he received a call from producer Norman Felton.

"He told me about U.N.C.L.E.—the overall conception, the ideas, the characters. I read a pilot script and that was enough for me." In describing his views on U.N.C.L.E., looking back on it years later, Vaughn observed, "I have nothing against it. In fact, it's a rather good charade and nobody is pretending it's more than that. The show is all right if you realize it's a massive put-on."

Vaughn was overwhelmed by the initial popularity of the series, which included thirty thousand fan letters per month. Regarding the fans he said, "In crowds they become uncontrollable and dangerous, otherwise they're well-meaning and considerate. I love them, even the dangerous ones." He went on to describe U.N.C.L.E. as, "A labor of love, tiring but very rewarding—both monetarily and professionally." Vaughn never looked down on the tangible achievements which accompanied success, stating, "If money is the root of all evil, then I want a bigger garden!"

A MAN NAMED SOLO

Initially Solo was just that, an agent who worked alone, and that's how he was portrayed in the pilot story for THE MAN FROM U.N.C.L.E., although it wasn't yet called that. Sam Rolfe created an 80 page outline for SOLO, and from that he wrote the pilot script, which was the only script Rolfe actually wrote for the series. Titled "The Vulcan Files," the first draft script was completed in June 1963 and when the final draft was turned in during November 1963, it was given production number 1059 by MGM Television. THE MAN FROM U.N.C.L.E. was about to be the first show out of the gate in the James Bond inspired espionage boom of the mid sixties.

As the pilot, now titled "The Vulcan Affair," opens, THRUSH and U.N.C.L.E. are already established and yet another skirmish between them is about to take place. Del Floria's tailor shop, the secret entrance to U.N.C.L.E. headquarters, is breached by THRUSH agents who manipulate the secret controls and enter U.N.C.L.E. HQ. Besides being a fast paced action scene, this also immediately introduces the viewer to some of the basic elements of the U.N.C.L.E. series.

We're shown Del Floria's, the secret entrance, as well as the massive interior of U.N.C.L.E. headquarters itself. The fact that the THRUSH agents don't know the security measures required to get very far without setting off alarms throughout the structure is also immediately established.

Badges are needed to gain access to the corridors beyond the reception area. While "The Vulcan Affair" showed that a black badge was required, the series would change this to a white badge to gain entry to the first floor, and later this would be changed to a yellow badge. Apparently for security reasons. The corridors and connecting rooms are all sealed with no windows opening onto the outside, except in the office of Mr. Waverly, the head of the New York branch of U.N.C.L.E.

ENTER THAT MAN FROM U.N.C.L.E.

"The Vulcan Affair" introduces Solo in an intriguing manner. A THRUSH agent sees the silhouette of a man in the hallway ahead of him. He opens fire and the very air seems to crack as a spider web pattern forms ahead of him—the THRUSH agent had been shooting at a wall of bullet-resistant glass. Solo then runs through a maze which protects him from further gunfire until he can get the drop on the THRUSH agent. The dramatic manner in which Solo is introduced establishes him as the character around whom the adventure will flow. That image of Napoleon Solo standing behind the spider-web of cracks would be repeated in a number of the episodes in the first season beginning with the eighth episode. Other early episodes have a prologue presenting the background of U.N.C.L.E. and the main characters in a pre-title sequence.

Illya is introduced right after we meet Napoleon Solo, but he's not established as Solo's comrade in arms right away. In fact in the first episode he only has a few lines and Solo goes it alone on the mission Waverly sends him on. In the first season of U.N.C.L.E., a number of plots involved U.N.C.L.E. recruiting a civilian to be a front for them on their missions. Often this civilian had some element in their background that enabled them to get access to the person U.N.C.L.E. wanted to deal with. By employing the civilian (who was asked to participate out of their patriotic duty), there would be nothing tying this person to U.N.C.L.E. since they'd never heard of the organization before meeting Napoleon Solo. Solo would sometimes make a reference to the organization as being his "uncle" in a manner which would make one think that he was talking about the United States government in the person of "Uncle Sam."

In the pilot we get a rare glimpse of Solo's apartment, which the script describes as having "touches that give one the impression that Solo is a seaman." Whether this is supposed to mean that Napoleon once served in some maritime branch of the armed services isn't revealed.

THE TRIUMPH OF THRUSH?

After U.N.C.L.E. was canceled midway through its

fourth season, Vaughn chose not to immediately rush into another series. As he explained it, "The first thing which happens when you do a successful series and go off the air is that everyone in town wants you to do the very same series with a different name, right away. I was pitched many, many deals by the networks and studios to do a series which would have been identical to U.N.C.L.E. But I wanted, since I wasn't married at the time, to travel and live in Europe and do movies. Therefore I didn't take advantage of my hotness after U.N.C.L.E."

THE MAN FROM U.N.C.L.E. aired from September 22, 1964 through January 15, 1968. Vaughn went to Europe after U.N.C.L.E. was canceled but still made a variety of motion pictures during the late sixties such as BULLITT (1968), THE BRIDGE AT REMAGEN (1969), THE MIND OF MR. SOAMES (1970), JULIUS CAESAR (1970), THE STATUE (1971) and CLAY PIGEON (1971). Besides film work, Vaughn wrote a book called ONLY VICTIMS which was published in 1972. The book dealt with the Hollywood blacklist of the early 1950's and the lives and careers it destroyed.

Then he was approached by a British production company to star in an adventure series which would be filmed in Europe and syndicated in the United States. It was called THE PROTECTORS. It was produced by Gerry Anderson, whose work until then had been on science fiction puppet shows like THUNDERBIRDS and CAPTAIN SCARLET.

THE CLONE OF SOLO

It's odd that Vaughn would turn down other U.N.C.L.E. clones and then in 1972 star in 52 episodes of THE PROTECTORS in which he played Harry Rule, a Napoleon Solo clone. Vaughn starred with Nyree Dawn Porter (as Contessa de Contini) and Tony Anholt (as Paul Buchet) as European crime fighters. Since many U.N.C.L.E. adventures took place in Europe, it all looked pretty familiar. Vaughn complained later that the series was pretty thin and he wouldn't do anything similar again, but the real problem in the series came from the scripts.

For an adventure series, THE PROTECTORS wasn't very exciting. It was distinctly unimaginative and one episode blurred dreamily into the next so that, in retrospect they became indistinguishable. It was as though the production company believed that the series would sell on the strength of the premise and the star. But viewers have to find a show interesting to watch, and when it is only 30 minutes long then it better deliver on the goods fast.

THE PROTECTORS tended to be all sizzle, but there was nothing in the pan. As good as it was to see Robert Vaughn as a Napoleon Solo clone just five years after U.N.C.L.E. was canceled (and I have nothing against an actor repeating the same type of character he's done well in the past), the stories just didn't give Vaughn's character anything interesting to do.

Like all too many European-made series of the '70s, the pacing of THE PRO- TECTORS was all too leisurely, which was odd considering '60s British shows like THE AVENGERS and THE CHAM- PIONS which seemed to know exactly what American audi- ences liked to watch. Even THE PRISONER, which could never be accused of being an action show, at least kept you interest- ed because it was something different every time. THE PRO- TECTORS tended to do the same plot over and over again.

It's no wonder the show flopped in the United States, which was too bad. It could have been a contender. Instead it's just an also-ran and a minor footnote in television history.

HEROES AND VILLAINS

Regarding THE PROTEC- TORS, Vaughn once remarked, "Apart from a little series I made in England, I was never again asked to be a romantic leading man. I went back to playing villains or politicians or white-collar mercenaries. It's more fun being a villain."

In an interview with Lee Goldberg in the May 1983 issue of STARLOG, Vaughn com- mented on the fact that inspite of having played a hero in four seasons of a TV series, he was inevitably thereafter cast in the role of the villain in film after film.

"For 10 years I played vil- lains predominantly before doing U.N.C.L.E. Once U.N.C.L.E. was over, I returned to playing villains and I have been for the last 15 years. There's been no conscious design about it. I keep getting offered those parts. But you can't be more villainous than trying to kill Superman in SUPERMAN III. It makes me the worst villain who ever lived. And my little boy, who is six years of age, is going to have to live that down in school every day."

In the July 1983 PREVUE Vaughn added, "I've never played another role like Napoleon Solo in the last 15 years and, in fact, I've done very few heroes. To me, villains are more interesting than heroes because they're usually more complex personalities. Richard Nixon is more complicated than Calvin Coolidge."

In 1982 writer/producer Michael Sloan made a deal with MGM which allowed him to revive U.N.C.L.E. as a movie made for television. Sloan met with McCallum in New York and he agreed to play Illya again if Vaughn would agree to play Solo. In Los Angeles, Sloan met with Vaughn who agreed to play Solo if McCallum would agree to play Illya Kuryakin. With the two actors attached to the project, Sloan was able to get a commitment from CBS and then everything else fell into place.

Regarding how he looked on playing Solo again, Vaughn explained, "I've always played myself in the role, and I'm just playing myself again—but 15 years older."

THE 15 YEARS LATER AFFAIR

"I'm glad to be back in the ring," Vaughn told PREVUE in the July 1983 issue. "I guess I've missed the need to constantly look over my shoulder—for booby traps in my Fruit-of-the-Loom underwear—and the thrill of knowing someone wants to kill me. As they say, 'Once a spy, always a spy!' I may be older, but my reflexes are remarkably sharp, and I cherish the thought of battling Mr. Vaselavitch again. This time, he must be stopped. No! He will be stopped because otherwise the peace of the nation—possibly the entire universe—will be threatened! Besides, I have a very wealthy aunt living in Chicago."

At the time he was making RETURN OF THE MAN FROM U.N.C.L.E.: THE 15 YEARS LATER AFFAIR, Vaughn expressed a willingness to return to the grind of a weekly series should the U.N.C.L.E. movie prove popular enough to spin-off a new series.

"Yes, I would," said Vaughn, "for the simple reason that I'm tired of foreign locations; Europe, Yugoslavia, Australia and god knows where else. I'm never with my family and it would give me a chance to be with them in America. Yes, I welcome the idea of a series, but this series, not any series.

"I'll be glad to do another, but only if I can work a deal to stay in the east and not relocate my family to Los Angeles. I remember driving up to my son's school in L.A. some years ago and everyone else had Lincolns and Rolls Royces. I thought, 'This is no place to raise a child in.' I was driving a Cadillac."

RETURN OF THE MAN FROM U.N.C.L.E. was interesting as far as it went, but was plagued by budgetary restrictions, rewriting which removed much of the true U.N.C.L.E. flavor from the storyline (including a canceled flashback sequence which was key to this aspect of the film) and editing which cut out the special U.N.C.L.E. touches which had been shot. It wasn't a bad film, but neither was it all that it could have been. [See the chapter elsewhere in this book on the behind-the-scenes story of THE RETURN OF THE MAN FROM U.N.C.L.E.]

SOLO NO MORE

When the ratings for RETURN OF THE MAN FROM U.N.C.L.E. were not strong enough to convince CBS to pick it up as a series, Vaughn returned to acting in episodic TV and the occasional motion picture. At the Emmy Awards presented on September 17, 1978, Vaughn won for Outstanding Continuing Performance By A Supporting Actor In A Drama Series for WASHINGTON: BEHIND CLOSED DOORS.

In the summer of 1993 Robert Vaughn was the host of DANGER THEATER, a show which was a parody of action adventure programs. In one segment, Vaughn even began to wax nostalgic about having once been the man from U.N.C.L.E.

Now 61, nostalgia may well be the only connection Vaughn will ever again have to Napoleon Solo as the recently announced motion picture revival of THE MAN FROM U.N.C.L.E. will undoubtedly recast the primary roles with younger performers. Since the producers will be hoping that U.N.C.L.E. will become an ongoing motion picture series just as STAR TREK and James Bond have been, they'll be hedging their bets by employing actors who are close to that magic age of 30 so that they'll be able to play the roles for many years to come. Robert

Vaughn was 31 when he first stepped into the role of Napoleon Solo, and the rigors of espionage (and a motion picture series) demand that youth be among the first considerations.

But Robert Vaughn made such an indelible impression as Napoleon Solo that any other actor will have a difficult time equaling, much less overcoming, that lingering celuloid image.

When THE MAN FROM U.N.C.L.E. began, Illya was an exotic secondary character who was quickly elevated in status based on an enthusiastic viewer reaction to him. This phenomenon was very similar to what would happen two years later on a TV show called STAR TREK with another exotic secondary character named Spock.

Chapter Five

ILLYA KURYAKIN: FROM RUSSIA WITH LOVE

Originally, THE MAN FROM U.N.C.L.E. of the title was Napoleon Solo. In the pilot episode, "The Vulcan Affair," Illya Kuryakin appears briefly early in the story but has only a few lines. It was clear from his initial appearance, though, that Illya was Russian. Because of that the character was almost cut from the show.

When NBC executives saw the pilot, they told Felton to lose "the chief." The producer naturally assumed that they wanted him to replace the actor who played the head of U.N.C.L.E. when actually they had been referring to Illya. Why they would refer to Illya as "the chief" is unknown. By the time the error had been realized, Leo G. Carroll had been cast as Mr. Waverly and David McCallum had been elevated to being the co-star of the series. Probably the fact that McCallum was a British actor playing the role of a Russian is all that initially saved his character on the show.

David McCallum was born on the 19th of September in 1933. His parents were professional musicians, his mother a concert cellist and his father the lead violinist for the London Philharmonic. In an interview published in the NEW YORK TIMES for October 24, 1965, the actor was quoted as recalling, "Naturally they thought it would be quite filial if I devoted myself to the oboe. I wanted to oblige them, but it was not to be."

His acting career began after he secured a job in a Glasgow theater as an electrician's helper when he was 14. McCallum appeared on BBC television in juvenile roles and later studied at the Royal Academy of Dramatic Arts in London. His stage career was interrupted by a stint in the British Army when he was stationed in Ghana.

THE TELEVISION CREDITS OF ILLYA KURYAKIN

Series
THE INVISIBLE MAN (1975-76)
COLDITZ
KIDNAPPED (1978)
SAPPHIRE AND STEEL (1979-82)

Guest Appearances — Original air date
SIR FRANCIS DRAKE: "The English Dragon" (Sept. 2, 1962)
THE OUTER LIMITS: "The Sixth Finger" (Oct. 14, 1963)
THE TRAVELS OF JAIMIE McPHEETERS: "The Day of the Search"
                                 (Jan. 19, 1964)
PERRY MASON: "The Case of the Fifty Millionth Frenchman"
                                 (Feb. 20, 1964)
THE OUTER LIMITS: "The Form of Things Unknown" (May 4, 1964)
THE GREAT ADVENTURE: "Kentucky's Bloody Ground"
                        (2 parts, April 3 and April 10, 1964)
THE ANDY WILLIAMS SHOW (April 20, 1965)
HULLABALLOO (Sept. 20, 1965)
THE FESTIVAL OF THE ARTS (Nov. 5, 1965)
PLEASE DON'T EAT THE DAISIES: "Say Uncle" (Nov. 11, 1966)
HALLMARK HALL OF FAME: "Teacher, Teacher" (Feb. 5, 1969)
                 "The File on Devlin" (Nov. 21, 1969)
NIGHT GALLERY: "The Phantom Farmhouse" (Oct. 20, 1971)
THE MAN AND THE CITY: "Pipe Me A Loving Tune" (Dec. 8, 1971)
MARCUS WELBY: "Just A Little Courage" (Feb. 15, 1972)
THE SIX MILLION DOLLAR MAN: "Wine, Women and War"
                                 (Oct. 20, 1973)
BERT D'ANGELO, SUPERSTAR: "A Noise in the Street"
                                (March 27, 1976)
STRIKE FORCE: "Ice" (Jan. 15, 1982)
HART TO HART: "Hunted Harts" (Jan. 4, 1983)
AS THE WORLD TURNS (Aug. 26, 1983 to Oct. 25, 1983)
THE MASTER: "Hostage" (Feb. 17, 1984)
BABYLON 5 (1994)

Feature Films (* indicates an U.N.C.L.E. feature film)
DANGEROUS YEARS (1956)
THE SECRET PLACE (1956)
JUNGLE STREET GIRLS/JUNGLE STREET (1957)
ROBBERY UNDER ARMS (1957)
VIOLENT PLAYGROUND (1958)
A NIGHT TO REMEMBER (1961)
THE LONG, THE SHORT AND THE TALL/JUNGLE FIGHTERS (1962)
BILLY BUDD (1962)
FREUD/THE SECRET PASSION (1962)
THE GREAT ESCAPE (1963)
THE GREATEST STORY EVER TOLD (1965)
AROUND THE WORLD UNDER THE SEA (1966)
TO TRAP A SPY (1966)*
THE SPY WITH MY FACE (1966)*
ONE SPY TOO MANY (1966)*
ONE OF OUR SPIES IS MISSING (1966)*
THE BIG TNT SHOW (1966)

THREE BITES OF THE APPLE (1967)
THE SPY IN THE GREEN HAT (1967)*
THE KARATE KILLERS (1967)*
THE HELICOPTER SPIES (1968)*
HOW TO STEAL THE WORLD (1968)*
SOL MADRID (1968)
THE RAVINE (1969)
MOSQUITO SQUADRON (1969)
HAUSER'S MEMORY (1973)(TV movie)
ESCAPE FROM COLDITZ (1972)
SHE WAITS (1972)(TV movie)
THE SCREAMING SKULL (1973)(TV movie)
FRANKENSTEIN: THE TRUE STORY (1973)(TV movie)
DOGS (1976)
THE KINGFISHER CAPER (1976)
KING SOLOMON'S TREASURE (1978)
THE WATCHER IN THE WOODS (1981)
CRITICAL LIST (1981)
BEHIND ENEMY LINES (1985)(TV movie)

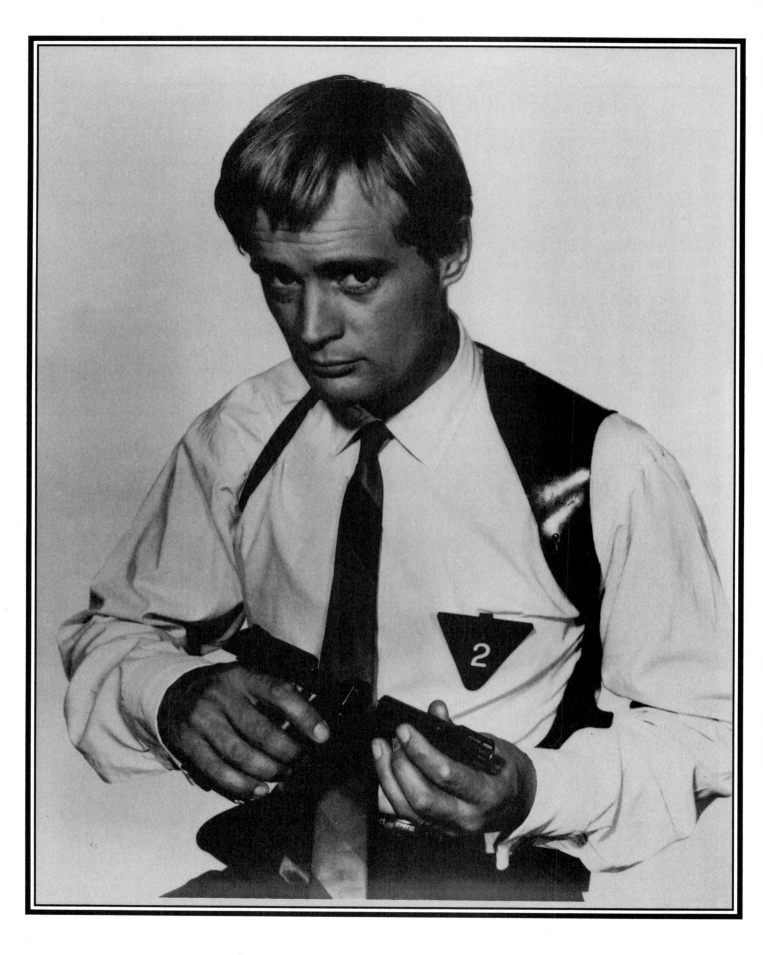

ALL THE SPIES

His early movie work includes the 1956 film HELL DRIVERS. That film also features some soon to be up-and-coming British actors such as Sean Connery, Patrick McGoohan, Jill Ireland (David's first wife) and William Hartnell, forever immortalized as the first actor to ever play Dr. Who.

McCallum has positive memories of HELL DRIVERS. "It is a fascinating film because Sean Connery, David McCallum, and Patrick McGoohan were in that film. When it was released in this country for television they cut me out! If you get the original HELL DRIVERS and take a look at the cast it is quite fascinating."

In the 1960's he appeared in A NIGHT TO REMEMBER, about the maiden voyage of the Titanic. Other early '60s films include BILLY BUDD and THE GREAT ESCAPE.

A year before U.N.C.L.E., in the fall of 1963, David McCallum was the featured guest star on a very memorable episode of THE OUTER LIMITS titled "The Sixth Finger." In it David played a Welsh minor who volunteers for an evolution experiment in order to earn some extra money. A machine succeeds in stimulating his evolutionary processes until he becomes what human beings will be a million years from now. McCallum gave a sensitive and bravura performance. McCallum suggested a scene in which his character learns to play the piano by reading books overnight, which required that David learn some simple pieces on the piano since he is seen actually playing it in the episode when the camera pans from his fingers up to his face.

SCIENCE FICTION CLASSIC

One complicating factor in playing the piano in "The Sixth Finger" was the fact that his character actually has six fingers on each hand by the time this scene takes place. "Joe Stefano wrote the dialogue where Gwyllm talks about it being a simple matter of mathematics and manual dexterity. But you try playing the piano with six fingers some time. It's not that easy!" he recalled later in an interview in THE OUTER LIMITS: THE OFFICIAL COMPANION. McCallum also appeared in another episode, "The Forms of Things Unknown," which aired in May 1964.

George Pal was so impressed by McCallum's eerie performance in "The Sixth Finger" that he cast him as the lead in the science fiction film he was then preparing titled ODD JOHN, based on the classic Olaf Stapledon novel. But the project came apart and the film was never made.

In 1964 McCallum played Judas in THE GREATEST STORY EVER TOLD, which was released the following year when he was already co-starring in THE MAN FROM U.N.C.L.E. In an interview published in TOP SECRET #3 (April, 1986), McCallum revealed to David Caruba how he came to be cast as Illya Kuryakin.

"Charles Bronson and I were in the commissary of MGM and I met Don Medford, who was directing it, and they were looking for someone to play the part. I spoke with Norman Felton, the producer, and he asked me to do it. It was just being at the right place at the right time."

A film he made during his off-season time from U.N.C.L.E. was the adventure AROUND THE WORLD UNDER THE SEA. In the April 1966 issue of SKIN DIVER magazine, McCallum stated, "It was a tremendous experience diving to great depths and see-ing the amazing marine life. Although I had never skin dived as had Bridges and Kelly in their TV series, I insisted on doing all my own underwater stunts."

U.N.C.L.E. BEGINS

Jill Ireland appeared in two episodes of U.N.C.L.E. during the course of the series. David's marriage to her was already breaking up in 1964, but the divorce wasn't final until 1966. They had three children togeth-er—Valentine, Jason and Paul. Paul has also become an actor, appearing in such '80s films as 10 TO MIDNIGHT and DEATHWISH II. Jill married Charles Bronson and later fought a losing battle with can-cer which claimed her life in 1992. In 1967 McCallum mar-ried Katherine Carpenter with whom he had two children, Peter and Sophie.

In "The Vulcan Affair," the character of Illya was clearly a secondary role. "When I began to play Illya, the character was little more than a lackey with a suppressed sneeze." But the character was quickly expand-ed until he became Napoleon Solo's right hand man. Billed as a co-star in season one, from season two on McCallum had equal billing with Vaughn.

Illya, even though he was an agent of U.N.C.L.E. just like Napoleon Solo, always seemed like Solo's opposite. He was light where Solo was dark; taciturn where Solo was talkative; remote where Solo was accessible. But at the time David McCallum had his own explanation for Illya's immediate popularity with viewers.

"Illya appeals mostly to the teenage U.N.C.L.E. fans. He is a loner. There is something real, real mystical about him. He is the man in black and has a carefree take-it-or-leave-it attitude. I think all this really appeals to the younger generation. Illya became a sex symbol. At first it was disquieting to me with my Calvinistic background and stiff Scottish spine. But now I find it very gratifying."

WHO IS ILLYA?

David McCallum isn't the kind of actor who just reads his lines, but rather he wanted to add some elements of characterization as well. "I introduced a note of friction between him and Napoleon. I thought a little animosity would add interest." It was also his idea that little would be known about Illya's background.

McCallum had done this before in THE OUTER LIMITS episode "The Sixth Finger." One of his lines was supposed to be: "It is the goal of evolution; Man's final destiny is to become what he imagined in the beginning when he first learned the idea of the angels." Said McCallum, "I changed one word from the script and it had to do directly with the religious aspect of the show. I changed it to 'first dreamed the idea,' because it was as if Gwyllm was talking scientifically about angels and I felt that was totally wrong. I was reprimanded by having to change it back, and if you listen, you'll notice that one line is dubbed in."

AMERICANIZATION OF U.N.C.L.E.

Although McCallum chose to keep Illya's history a secret, he complicated it by keeping his weeding ring on during filming.

"I wear it because I'm married and feel thoroughly married and value that feeling. When I began to play Illya, I simply forgot to remove that ring. Pretty soon letters were cascading in by the hundreds asking what sort of woman Illya was married to, how many kids he had, where and why he kept his family locked off-stage and so on. My reaction was, and happily our producers agreed, why spell out Illya's background? Why not leave the wedding ring and never say a mumbling word about it?"

In describing U.N.C.L.E. he states, "There's definitely an American aspect to the show. You have such an aggressive, imaginative society in this country. What amazes me is that you're only four centuries old. You achieve more in less time than is accomplished in Europe where everything's a thousand years old. In England U.N.C.L.E. would be considered a liberal show. I used to get letters saying, 'How dare you play a Russian?' Then came the 'we-love-you-anyway' notes. Now I get 'Dear Illya, you may be a communist, but you're our communist.' "

During the third season of U.N.C.L.E., Illya no longer spoke with an accent, an acting decision that McCallum defended.

"He had been in America for a number of years. Anyone who has an accent who lives in a country for a number of years—that's what happens to them. It was just a natural development."

THE RETURN OF U.N.C.L.E.

Although he is more interested in discussing his more recent work and these days will discuss U.N.C.L.E. only with great reluctance, McCallum admits that U.N.C.L.E. was, "probably the most delightful time I've had in my career." He liked working with Robert Vaughn and Leo G. Carroll and didn't think that U.N.C.L.E. typecast him at all.

"The truth is I haven't played a Russian spy since then. Perhaps there were producers who said, 'I'd like somebody like David to play this part, but I don't want him because he's too identified as Illya Kuryakin.' But on the positive side I haven't stopped working as an actor since 1947."

Regarding whether he thought that U.N.C.L.E. would be successful when he started it, McCallum stated, "I didn't think along those terms. I was just glad to get the check. When it became successful it was a bonus."

In the '70s and '80s McCallum worked in a variety of TV series including THE INVISIBLE MAN (from 1975-76), KIDNAPPED (1978), SAPPHIRE & STEEL (1979-82) and another British series called COLDITZ in which he starred with Robert Wagner.

On the set of RETURN OF THE MAN FROM U.N.C.L.E., McCallum was interviewed but was reluctant to talk specifically about U.N.C.L.E. although he stated that he was not at all reluctant to do the reunion film. "I don't think in those terms of escaping or coming back," he told Lee Goldberg. "Working is working and if it's a good script and a good part and the right time, then it's a pleasure."

When asked his opinion about the trend to do remakes of old TV series, McCallum stated, "I don't feel anything about trends in television. They call me in. I act the part to the best of my ability, they give me a check, and I go home. And now you're writing all that down as if I just came out and said it. That's the problem with interviews. I had never even considered the subject. You are totally distorting my life by doing this. I don't mean to be difficult, but I wouldn't say anything about trends. That's the problem with interviews."

SAPPHIRE AND STEEL

McCallum was more willing to discuss the other TV series he appeared in, such as SAPPHIRE AND STEEL, in which he starred with Joanna Lumley.

"We played a couple who put things right wherever there was a tear in the fabric of time. Joanna told me there was some interest in doing a feature version of SAPPHIRE AND STEEL, but I haven't heard anything about it yet. We had some marvelous scripts. I used to have a hard time explaining the show. Did you see POLTERGEIST? SAPPHIRE AND STEEL is POLTERGEIST. The same sort of story."

But he admits that it wouldn't have played well in the United States.

"No, it was done on tape, for one thing, with out of date cameras. I just don't feel that particular kind of heavy-edited British television works over here. I think that subject over here would have been done on film and it would have been done like TWILIGHT ZONE. It would have been slicker. By doing it on tape, editing it in the camera as you shoot and not really re-editing it or tightening it up, they were a bit laborious compared to what they're used to here."

He had less kind remarks for THE INVISIBLE MAN which he felt derailed after the pilot was made and it became a short-lived (4 months) series on NBC.

THE FUTURE

Regarding U.N.C.L.E., McCallum has tended to be

reluctant to discuss it at length, perhaps because he played a character in an action adventure show which involved little, if any, real dramatic acting. When the actor is drawn into conversation about U.N.C.L.E., he tends to speak in generalities, dismissing specific questions about the series.

"I think it stands up very well," McCallum remarked after watching some episodes in the mid-eighties when it was syndicated to cable TV. "MGM has done a wonderful job on the negatives—they come out looking very clean and beautiful. Some of them are real dogs! You do 104 shows, you can't expect them all to be great."

Although McCallum had been willing to be a part of a new series had THE RETURN OF THE MAN FROM U.N.C.L.E. been a bigger hit in 1983, a few years later, after U.N.C.L.E. was syndicated to cable television, he had changed his mind.

"I don't think I want to do any more U.N.C.L.E.'s," he told David Caruba at TOP SECRET magazine. "Having seen the fact that MGM has 100 of them that are going out one a night on CBN, it's crazy. So I think no, I don't want to do that ever again."

Chapter Six

THRUSH AND U.N.C.L.E.'S ENEMIES

The name of this evil organization was actually still up in the air when THE MAN FROM U.N.C.L.E. was being developed. For one thing, NBC executives apparently preferred the name WASP until they discovered that there was a real group with that name. Early pre-production scripts, such as the one for "The Four Steps Affair," used a different name: MAGGOT, which would probably have been an even nastier organization.

At one point, Norman Felton asked his staff to devise alternative names. They came up with a wide and wild variety of evil sobriquets: HYENA, VISION, RAVEN, ROACH, SPIDER, the oddly unthreatening GUMPS, ALGAE, and SHROUD. The best of the lot was SQUID, if only for the words that comprised it: Society for Quiet Unification through International Destruction! Likewise, it seems as if the idea behind THRUSH took some time to develop as the series progressed.

In the very first episode, "The Vulcan Affair," Napoleon Solo offered the following thoughts on the nemesis that would bedevil him and Illya Kuryakin for the next three and a half years:

"THRUSH might be a man. . . Or a woman. . . Or a committee of some sort. THRUSH is the head of a secret international organization. . . very powerful, very wealthy. THRUSH has no allegiance to any culture nor any ideal. It will embark on any undertaking which THRUSH may decide is in its own interest. And where THRUSH succeeds, many, many people pay a terrible price."

WHAT IS THRUSH?

At this point, it seems that no one really knew exactly what THRUSH really was. But soon enough, it became apparent that it was an evil organization owing much to groups like Ian Fleming's

SMERSH, but without any distinct national background. Or, more precisely, Fleming's SPECTRE, a criminal group of some sort rather than the spy apparatus of any foreign government.

After a few weak forays (note their botched raid on U.N.C.L.E. in "The Vulcan Affair"), THRUSH began to come into its own, using killer toy robots and surgically altered doubles in its war on U.N.C.L.E. Soon enough, special THRUSH weapons and uniforms began to be seen as well.

The true character of the organization was finally and firmly established in the first-season episode "The Deadly Decoy," in which THRUSH agents again raided U.N.C.L.E. Headquarters. This time around, they were armed with special weapons. The people behind the show obviously considered this an important step in the evolution of THRUSH, because they went so far as to have Napoleon Solo address the audience in the teaser with a few words about the nemesis they were about to see in action!

Like U.N.C.L.E., THRUSH had its own sections, which for some reason included exclamation points in their nomenclature:

Ultimate Computer Force: Plotting and Scheming!
Intelligence Force: Mind Warpage and Information!
Assault Force: Death, Torture, Terror!
Anti-Personnel Force: Identity Alteration and Hazardous Duty!
Self-Destruct Squad: Doomsday Missions!

Perhaps THRUSH just took itself a bit too seriously for its own good!

THE SECRETS OF THRUSH

Like U.N.C.L.E., THRUSH had a background organization that was discussed very little in the series. Thrush's branch offices were known as Satraps. (At one point, U.N.C.L.E. is alarmed to discover that the New York Satrap is six blocks away from Del Floria's tailor shop!) The main Headquarters was known as the City Of THRUSH, a mobile city with its own banking, police force, government, military and scientists.

The logistics of the City of THRUSH must have been staggering, and certainly beyond the limits of the show's budget. The City housed the Ultimate

Computer (which wasn't ultimate enough to get the drop on Solo or Illya) and the Supreme Council, the top dozen (or so) THRUSH members. Together, the Council and the Computer ran things— and the computer even got its name in an episode title: second season's "The Ultimate Computer Affair." The City was never mentioned on the show, but was always referred to as THRUSH Central.

As THE MAN FROM U.N.C.L.E. progressed, more came to light about their arch-enemy. The THRUSH insignia showed up late in the first season. Later, uniforms, custom weapons and technology, and a more concrete identity were added as well.

Sam Rolfe, in many ways the real creator of both THE MAN FROM U.N.C.L.E. series and the background of THRUSH, left at the end of the first season. An ensuing lack of focus began to develop in the show, which would manifest itself in the camp elements which would swamp the series during the third season.

THRUSH was perhaps at its best when Rolfe was still around. Afterwards, it became a generic villain, often giving the writers an excuse to avoid devising any real interesting villainous characters. Dr.

Egret, the faceless woman villain, was only used twice, once in "The Mad, Mad Tea Party Affair" and again in "The Girls of Nazarone Affair." The freelance Gervaise Ravel also showed up twice, played by Anne Francis both times. THRUSH Doctor Dabree was played by Elsa Lanchester in "The Brain Killer Affair," wearing her BRIDE OF FRANKENSTEIN makeup all over again. But even without Rolfe, THRUSH was still the main threat to world order. "The Adriatic Express Affair" mentioned the origin of THRUSH: it was formed in February 1923, by one Olga Nemirovitch, a cosmetic mogul!

THRUSH IN PRINT

When in doubt, fake it. This seems to have been the principle which guided U.N.C.L.E. paperback author David McDaniel. He wrote what many consider the best of the MAN FROM U.N.C.L.E. novels— and made up his own back history for THRUSH. According to McDaniel, THRUSH was an acronym for Technological Hierarchy for the Removal of Undesirables and the Subjugation of Humanity. The origin: in 1895, THRUSH was founded by Sherlock

Holmes' arch-enemy, Professor Moriarity! This, courtesy of the head of THRUSH himself, who tells all this to Illya and Solo when THRUSH and U.N.C.L.E. must team up to save the world from a third group. Highly unlikely in the television version!

As can be seen, THRUSH was many things to many people. Perhaps this is the result of their highly effective disinformation campaigns, a screen to mask their true nature. Be that as it may, U.N.C.L.E. will always stand ready to combat them— whoever or whatever they are.

Chapter Seven

UNCLE GUEST STARS

Watching THE MAN FROM UNCLE, like watching so many other television programs from earlier decades, can be like a video history lesson, as actors on their way to fame, and famous folk now forgotten, appeared on it quite often. For instance, when William Shatner and Leonard Nimoy first appeared together on the same show, it was in "The Project Strigas Affair," a first season episode of THE MAN FROM UNCLE. Nimoy portrayed the rather dull witted assistant of an ambassador from a Eastern Bloc country, Kurasov. When U.N.C.L.E decides to put an end to Kurasov's threat to the West, they con him into believing that a new nerve gas is being developed.

Shatner played Mike Donfield, who is enlisted by U.N.C.L.E to be the man willing to sell the U.S. government's secret formula. When Kurasov uses a large sum of his nation's money to bribe Donfield, the trap is sprung— the formula is really one for floor wax! Kurasov is called home in disgrace. Kurasov, by the way, was played by another actor who did a lot of TV work during this period— Werner Klemperer, soon to assume his Emmy-winning role as Colonel Klink on the hit series HOGAN'S HEROES.

FUTURE SPIES

Some U.N.C.L.E guest stars would go on to star in their own spy shows. Robert Culp, about to team up with Bill Cosby on I, SPY, appeared in a very early episode: "The Shark Affair." Here he played Captain Shark, a latter-day pirate who is waging a strange battle to keep humanity alive. Obsessed by nuclear war, he is taking away people who answer his employment ads and adding them to the crew of his ship, which is designed to survive the nuclear war he believes to be inevitable. His crew will then repopulate the earth, The plot thickens when Shark begins kidnapping the families and loved ones of his crew off of cruise ships, leading U.N.C.L.E to the pirate, who nobly goes down with his ship in the end. This is also notable for a supporting role by James Doohan, sporting a British accent in this pre-Scotty role.

"The Never Never Affair" featured Barbara Feldon, the future Agent 99 of GET SMART. Here she plays a clerk in the Portuguese translation department of U.N.C.L.E who is given the wrong list when she's sent shopping for Waverly's tobacco. As a result, THRUSH's top French agent, played by Cesar Romero (soon to play the Joker on BATMAN), is quickly after her. The humor in this story, natural rather than forced as in later seasons, gave Feldon an opportunity to flex her comedic talents, and may very well have been a factor that led to her being cast as Don Adams' opposite number in the ultimate '60s spy parody.

The STAR TREK connection hit more than once, this time in the person of Roger C. Carmel, the ubiquitous character actor of the period. In "The Quadripartite Affair" he played Horth, a cigarette smuggler who helps out the men from U.N.C.L.E and Marion Raven only to be killed by minions of Gervaise Ravel. Carmel appeared on U.N.C.L.E. again as Captain Cervantes in "The Ultimate Computer Affair" during the second season.

FUTURE STARS

Future STAR TREK arch villain Ricardo Montalban also appeared in two episodes. His first MAN FROM U.N.C.L.E, "The Dove Affair," also featured June Lockhart, at the time known as a star of the LASSIE series which ran from 1958 to 1964, but soon to join the cast of LOST IN SPACE.

Lockhart plays an American tourist who is drawn into an U.N.C.L.E affair quite by chance (a lot of those around). Solo is trapped in an Eastern Bloc country after stealing a medallion from the body of its dictator as it lies in state! It contains the names of all the THRUSH agents in Europe. Unfortunately, THRUSH has bought out just about everybody in Sernia, making it rather hard to get out of the country. The only person Solo can trust is the chief of the secret police, Satine (Montalban), who has not been corrupted by THRUSH.

Rather than being a villain, Montalban's character was an honest adversary, willing to help Solo up to a point but more interested in getting the medallion himself in order to undo THRUSH's hold on his nation. In fact, in the end Satine gets the medallion, although Solo and the American tourists get out with a photo of the list as well.

Montalban made his second MAN FROM U.N.C.L.E guest shot in the second season episode "The King Of Diamonds Affair." Here he played Rafael Delgado, a suave diamond thief who U.N.C.L.E enlists to help solve some puzzling jewel thefts. What they don't know is that Delgado is behind the thefts himself, unhindered by imprisonment. Not quite as good as Montalban's first outing, this one is a fairly silly episode. While the third season of U.N.C.L.E. is often singled out for drubbing, the silly handwriting was already on the wall in year two. Year three just had a lot more of it.

Other famous guest stars included: Jack Lord ("The His Master's Touch Affair"), Vincent Price ("The Fox And Hounds Affair"), Jack Palance and Janet Leigh ("The Concrete Overcoat Affair"), George Sanders ("The Gazebo In The Maze Affair" and "The Yukon Affair") and Nancy Sinatra ("The Take Me To Your Leader Affair"). In addition to her two appearances as Marion Raven in "The Quadripartite Affair" and "The Giuoco Piano Affair," Jill Ireland (Mrs. David McCallum at the time) played different characters in "The Tigers Are Coming Affair" and "The Five Daughters Affair."

Yvonne Craig, Sonny & Cher, Victor Buono and Victor Borge also appeared. Watch enough MAN FROM UNCLE episodes and you're bound to see some familiar faces.

It is interesting to note that of the U.N.C.L.E. episodes released on tape and videodisc, the selections have not been at random (which would have found some excellent shows just through hit and miss) but by who the guest stars on a given episode are. Thus while the black and white "The Project Strigas Affair" was the first one released on tape, it was soon followed by "The Hot Number Affair," the third season episode with Sonny and Cher. Reportedly Sonny suffered a bloody nose in a fight scene when a punch thrown by McCallum accidentally connected. There are doubtless people who would have paid a lot of money to see that. Being a star just isn't what it used to be.

Chapter Eight

U.N.C.L.E. GOES TO THE MOVIES

With the spy craze generating big cinematic bucks all over the place in the early sixties, from the James Bond movies to such obscure classics as A DANDY IN ASPIC, it seemed pretty sensible to shoot a MAN FROM U.N.C.L.E. movie or two. In the true sense the word, of course, the only real theatrical U.N.C.L.E. movie will be the one currently in development. The U.N.C.L.E. movies of the period were episodes of the television show, with added footage, released in theaters.

The first U.N.C.L.E. movie, TO TRAP A SPY, was based on the MAN FROM U.N.C.L.E. pilot, "The Vulcan Affair." As discussed elsewhere, the head of U.N.C.L.E. in the pilot was one Mr. Allison, portrayed by veteran stage actor Will Kuluva. In the five months between the filming of this episode and the actual premiere of the series, Kuluva was replaced. However, producer Norman Felton had convinced MGM that a theatrical version for European and foreign release would make back some money, and the movie version retained the Allison character. And although the pilot was aired in black and white, it had been filmed in color— again, for purposes of theatrical release.

But the pilot, minus commercials and titles, ran about forty-seven minutes. Hardly a decent length for a theatrical film. Retaining the cut footage, and taking three days to shoot some extra footage, the production company put together an eighty-minute film. In this version, U.N.C.L.E.'s evil rival organization was named WASP, a name later changed for legal reasons.

THE DOWN SIDE OF THE FILMS

The unfortunate upshot of the U.N.C.L.E. movies is that most of the episodes which went to the big screen have been withheld from syndication. This also includes "The Four Steps Affair," an episode with an unusual history. The villainess, Luciana Paluzzi, was created for the footage filmed to pad out the movie TO TRAP A SPY. Ever resourceful, the producers then took that extra footage and built a TV episode around it, as well. "The Four Steps Affair" was aired only once, on February 22, 1965, and has rarely, if ever, been seen since.

The next MAN FROM U.N.C.L.E. feature film was THE SPY WITH MY FACE, based on "The Double Affair," first broadcast on November 17, 1964. Written by Clyde Ware and directed by John Newland, "The Double affair" was, again, filmed in color but shown in black and white by NBC. The reasons are twofold: NBC still had not gone to regular color transmissions— and they would have had to pay MGM/Arena about twenty per cent more to show the episode in color, anyway. This movie was adapted from a one-hour episode, so more extra footage was needed, and the character of Australian U.N.C.L.E. agent Kitt Kittredge (Donald Harron) was created for the added scenes. Kittredge had an unusual career even for an agent of U.N.C.L.E.— he was killed in THE SPY WITH MY FACE, but later returned as a one-shot character on the series (again through the judicious recycling of footage).

TV VERSUS MOVIE

In the television version of "The Double Affair," THRUSH readies their plan to replace Napoleon Solo with a lookalike, and try to get rid of Illya with a horde of murderous toy robots. This part of the plan fails, but Solo is easily caught thanks to the sexy THRUSH agent Serena. While the double joins Illya on a mission in Switzerland, the real Solo wakes to find himself imprisoned in Austria. (One nice touch: Solo's girlfriend, Sandy, thinks that Napoleon— really the double— is snubbing her, and spills hot coffee on him "accidentally on purpose" on the flight to Switzerland!)

Escaping, Solo converges with the fake, who is out to steal a new power source for THRUSH. Convenient air shafts and a well-timed explosion contribute to the success of our men from U.N.C.L.E. In a classic television battle (actually very well done) the two Solos duke it out, until Serena shoots one of them— the double. Accident, or—? Either way, Serena decides to face the music with her superiors at THRUSH, even though Solo tries to talk her out of it.

Unfortunately, the expansion of this storyline to feature length did not add anything to the viewability of this episode. If anything, it detracted from it. Napoleon Solo becomes incredibly lecherous in the movie version, in smarmy scenes featuring both the underwear-clad Sandy (Sharon Farrell) and the all-but-nude Serena (Senta Berger). The worst aspect of these scenes is the bad, double-entendre dialogue (single entendre, really) which attempts to capture the feel of the bond films. Senta Berger fans will enjoy the extra cleavage in the movie version, however.

The other extra footage featured Donald Harron as Kitt Kittridge, an Australian U.N.C.L.E. agent. In fact, the movie version starts with Kittridge, Solo and Kuryakin raiding a THRUSH base in Australia. Kittridge is the cover agent on the mission to Switzerland. He discovers that "Napoleon Solo" is a fake, but is killed for his pains. This leads to Illya's discovery of the impostor, and a near-fatal steambath engineered by Serena. In the episode version, Illya didn't know that Solo was a fake until he saw the doppelgangers together.

MORE FEATURES

The second season of THE MAN FROM U.N.C.L.E. was also the first year that NBC went to widespread color broadcasting. As a result of this, all U.N.C.L.E. episodes were now filmed in color. The series also began to feature two-part episodes, which made the transition of these episodes into feature films all that much simpler than before. The second season kicked off with a two-parter, "The Alexander The Greater Affair," which became the theatrical release ONE SPY TOO MANY. This would be the last MAN FROM U.N.C.L.E. feature to see release in the United States.

The remaining features would only hit screens in Europe, Asia and other foreign markets. This was due, most likely, to the poor box-office showing of ONE SPY TOO MANY; three U.N.C.L.E. features in two years, all of which must have seemed fairly familiar to anyone who'd seen the series version of each movie, must have oversaturated the market somewhat.

TO TRAP A SPY and THE SPY WITH MY FACE had done

good box-office, frequently as a double bill, but they may have been riding the crest of U.N.C.L.E.'s initial surge of popularity. While U.N.C.L.E. would maintain top ratings on television, its film career in its native country ended with ONE SPY TOO MANY.

Even though "The Alexander The Greater Affair" yielded a good ninety minutes of footage, extra scenes were still shot to add variation (and a bit more sex) to ONE SPY TOO MANY. Rip Torn played Alexander, an industrialist. He is determined, in the course of his quest to out-do Alexander the Great and conquer the world, to also break all of the ten commandments!

This will establish not only that he is a true conqueror, but also a really bad guy. Torn is in great form here. Fans of this Texas-born actor might be rather surprised to learn of his television work, but "The Alexander The Greater Affair," in either version, is made all the more enjoyable thanks to his performance.

DOWNHILL SLIDE

After this point, the movies become a bit weaker. ONE OF OUR SPIES IS MISSING, based on the already-befuddled "The Bridge Of Lions Affair," may have really broken the figurative camel's back as far as American release was concerned, despite stalwart work from British guest Maurice Evans, Bernard Fox, and Vera Miles.

"The Concrete Overcoat Affair" fared somewhat better when it was expanded into THE SPY IN THE GREEN HAT, which was limited to foreign release only. Here, Jack Palance is the over-the-top mobster villain, and Janet Leigh the heroine in distress. Veteran character actor Eduoardo Cianelli adds to the fun, as our heroes enlist the aid of local a Sicilian family (in every sense of the word) to defeat the Palance character.

Another foreign release, THE KARATE KILLERS, was based on "The Five Daughters Affair" from the third season. Oddly enough, the karate killers of the title were rather minor characters. With a cast that included Joan Crawford, Herbert Lom and Jill Ireland, this was a world-spanning tale with lots of exotic locales. The basic plot involved the search for the five daughters/step daughters of murdered scientist, Simon True.

Each daughter has a photograph of True with a piece of a puzzle on the back. Joining forces with his real daughter, Sandy, Napoleon Solo and Illya Kuryakin seek out the remaining four step daughters, a quest which takes them to Rome, London, Austria and Rio de Janeiro. Each stepdaughter seems to be in some sort of predicament, which our heroes must extricate them from. The puzzle, when assembled, leads them to Japan, where THRUSH Asia is developing a process to make gold. A new bit of U.N.C.L.E. tech surfaces here: Solo's shoe laces, when soaked in vinegar, become a potent explosive! As usual, yet another U.N.C.L.E. outing ends with a spectacular explosion.

THE END LOOKS UP

After THE HELICOPTER SPIES (foreign release only), based on "The Prince of Darkness Affair," the last U.N.C.L.E movie was based on the last two episodes of THE MAN FROM U.N.C.L.E. itself: HOW TO STEAL THE WORLD (foreign release only) was based on "The Seven Wonders Of The World Affair."

In this final affair, U.N.C.L.E.'s efforts to capture THRUSH chief Webb (Mark Richman) are foiled by Margitta, whose husband, Robert Kingsley, is an U.N.C.L.E. agent who has turned to work for THRUSH. This leads to the Himalayas, where THRUSH has kidnapped scientists to develop a docility gas. This was originally a single hour episode script padded out to two episodes. Norman Felton himself was unhappy with the episode, and felt it was a dismal send-off for THE MAN FROM U.N.C.L.E. Actually it isn't that bad as it recaptures the verve, style and action which made U.N.C.L.E. such a hit with the fans during its first season.

Felton may have been unhappy with it in looking back because of how violent it is. Felton subsequently tried to rewrite history, claiming that U.N.C.L.E. agents often used sleep darts in their guns rather than bullets—a facet virtually unknown in the series itself.

Most of the MAN FROM U.N.C.L.E. movies often turn up on television. Some, like HOW TO STEAL THE WORLD and ONE SPY TOO MANY, are really quite good, capturing the essence that made THE MAN FROM U.N.C.L.E. such an enduring legacy of sixties television.

Chapter Nine

THE ALL-TOO-COMPLICATED ELLISON AFFAIR

Renegade writer and firebrand, Harlan Ellison wrote a good deal for television during the early and mid 'sixties. It was inevitable that he wound up working on THE MAN FROM U.N.C.L.E. As might be expected by both fans and detractors of the perspicacious Ellison, controversy would eventually arise in regard to this aspect of his career.

Ellison's first association with The MAN FROM U.N.C.L.E. involved five uncredited script rewrites, which may have included "The Virtue Affair." His first official script, the third season's "The Sort Of Do-It-Yourself Dreadful Affair," was aired September 23, 1966. Directed by E. Darrell Hallenbeck, this affair has all the hallmarks of classic Ellison humor. Producer Norman Felton was a bit put off by Ellison's use of androids. He wanted to avoid science fiction at all costs. Actor Woodrow Parfrey, who appeared as five different characters during THE MAN FROM U.N.C.L.E.'s four-season run, played a character named Dr. Pertwee. This was Ellison's sly homage to Britain's DR. WHO.

THE DO-IT-YOURSELF DREADFUL AFFAIR

As the affair begins, Napoleon breaks into a THRUSH-operated pawn shop, only to be attacked by a young woman with seemingly superhuman strength and a zoned-out expression. Solo barely escapes the ordeal intact. Waverly, meanwhile, is perplexed: U.N.C.L.E. has evidence that THRUSH has over a billion dollars in assets, and is wondering why the evil organization is applying for a loan from a Swiss bank. When Napoleon and Illya stop to watch a sexy model filming a commercial (for "Spy Guy" lotion for men!), the zombie girl shows up again, only to be pursued by the model, Andy. The strange woman appears to be Muriel, an ex-roommate who owes Andy money.

Meanwhile, there is trouble at THRUSH Headquarters. Android A-77 has gone on the loose. THRUSH scientist Dr. Pertwee is ordered to set the android on self destruct. This saves Napoleon from another attack. Muriel collapses in mid-attack, and her secret is revealed. Our heroes investigate the fate of the real Muriel, the model for the android. Alas, the girl is dead, but not before serving as the model for an entire horde of androids, which Napoleon must face before the end of this tongue-in-cheek affair.

Napoleon poses as an officer of the Swiss bank, accompanied by Toffler, the real banker. Illya and Andy try to learn the fate of Muriel. Taken to THRUSH with blindfolds on, Napoleon and the banker learn why THRUSH needs another billion dollars: they are trying to build an invincible android army, which is obvious despite THRUSH man Lash's attempts to convince the bankers that the plan will benefit humanity.

When Andy and Illya learn of Muriel's death in a car acci-dent, they trace her posthumous trail to Pertwee, and are captured by THRUSH. Napoleon, meanwhile, tries to convince THRUSH that he wants to join them, and will convince the banker to approve the loan if he can. By wooing THRUSH femme fatale Margot, and getting her to turn off THRUSH's jamming devices so he can radio the bank, Napoleon manages to use his U.N.C.L.E. communicator as a homing beacon which allows U.N.C.L.E. to locate him.

Waverly is in for a bit of a shock. THRUSH's New York bureau is located a mere six blocks away from U.N.C.L.E.'s command center! (This is one of Ellison's funnier touches.) Illya, meanwhile, convinces Pertwee that THRUSH is evil—the somewhat befuddled scientist has been misled. THRUSH unleashes a horde of Muriel androids to kill our heroes, but Pertwee gives up his life to end their rampage, and THRUSH's latest shot at world domination.

PIECES OF FATE

Ellison's next script for THE MAN FROM U.N.C.L.E. was to be his last. An episode destined to join the ranks the great "lost" television programs of all time, at least for nearly 20 years it would.

"The Pieces Of Fate" affair (first aired February 24, 1967) took a thinly-veiled satirical shot at a real sitting duck: Jacqueline Suzanne, author of the trashy best-seller VALLEY OF THE DOLLS, became Jacqueline Midcult, author of a best selling novel called PIECES OF FATE. Napoleon and Illya attend a taping of the Joe White program (based on Joe Franklin, one of Ellison's pet peeves), on a mission from U.N.C.L.E.: it seems that the book is based on actual THRUSH cases, and U.N.C.L.E. is very, very curious about this— where did Midcult get her facts?

Oddly enough, Jacqueline Suzanne did not take action against this parody. Either she didn't care, didn't know about it, or had a better sense of humor than the person who would sue. This was Judith Merrill, represented by the character Judith Merle, a literary agent who is also a THRUSH agent. Merle kidnaps Midcult from a tea.

Meanwhile, THRUSH agents toss Illya and Napoleon down a coal chute, where they await certain doom when the coal is delivered. But wait— it's 1967, and the building converted to gas heating long before

this particular predicament. Another clever Ellison twist, inspired no doubt by his love for old movie serials.

THRUSH chief Zarko drugs Midcult and hypnotizes her, but she reverts to childhood (seven years, to be exact) and can only tell them that she has relatives in Painesville, Ohio. THRUSH heads to Painesville (Ellison's home town) with Midcult in tow, followed by Napoleon (who has Midcult bugged) and Illya. There they visit Buck's bookstore, where Buck, an acquaintance of Midcult's Uncle Charlie, has a manuscript of PIECES OF FATE. Outside the bookstore, Illya is kidnapped by Merle and a mysterious old man, but manages to escape with baffling ease.

Napoleon and Jacqueline go to see Uncle Charlie— who turns out to be Charles Coltrane, a THRUSH agent believed to be dead. Midcult used his diaries as her source. When she and Napoleon go to the attic to reclaim the diaries, they are attacked by Zarko and his thugs. Our heroes get the upper hand, only to be foiled by the arrival of Merle— who is foiled in turn by the old man with her, who turns out to be Waverly in disguise. The quest for the diaries is in vain, anyway. Charlie's wife, Midcult's

Aunt Jessie, had tossed them in the fire years ago.

TUCKERISMS

Ironically, Ellison did not raise the ire of his real satiric target, Jacqueline Suzanne. As an in-joke, he put in a number of friends and acquaintances from the science fiction world. This was trait used by science fiction writer Bob Tucker, which resulted in the deed being called a "Tuckerism" whenever anyone else perpetrated the joke.

Norman Spinrad lent his surname to a THRUSH enforcer, Buck was based on Jack Vance, and Merle was based on Judith Merrill, who sued MGM over this affair. Sour grapes, perhaps? After its initial airing, "The Pieces Of Fate Affair" pulled out of circulation, and was never been seen in syndication until Ted Turner acquired the MGM film and television library and began broadcasting U.N.C.L.E. on his cable networks in 1985.

When the episode did air (following a meager out of court settlement agreed to by Merrill), the name of the offending character had been redubbed so that she was now called "Jody Moore." The fact that the episode was never rerun between 1967 and 1985 caused some hard feelings to be sure as this meant that none of the participants received rerun residuals they ordinarily would have been paid in 1967.

Whether all this trouble was the reason that Ellison never wrote another MAN FROM U.N.C.L.E. script, or if he just moved on to other pastures, is unclear. For U.N.C.L.E. fans, this was long a major gap in the canon. For Harlan Ellison, it was just another intriguing footnote to his long creative career.

Chapter Ten

HIGH TECH, SIXTIES STYLE

As envisioned by Sam Rolfe, U.N.C.L.E. was a vast worldwide organization with considerable resources at its disposal. According to Rolfe, there were five headquarters for U.N.C.L.E. (as well as various local offices) around the world, but only three were ever mentioned on the show: Calcutta, Berlin, and New York. The New York office was the focus of the series,. and the entry to that headquarters was the first inkling that viewers had of the secret technologies that made U.N.C.L.E. tick.

The "front" office of U.N.C.L.E. is located in the building of a private dining club, The Mask Club. To the general public, U.N.C.L.E. seems to be an international charity of some sort, and will see nothing to dispel that belief unless they somehow make their way to a private lounge with an elevator that leads down to the real headquarters.

U.N.C.L.E. agents, on the other hand, use the famous entry through Del Floria's tailor shop, around the corner and down the block from The Mask Club. The tailor seems to be an U.N.C.L.E. agent with one function: triggering the secret button on his steam press that activates the hook on the back wall of the shop's sole fitting booth. Once he's done his duty, that hook can be turned to open the secret door in the fitting booth; otherwise, it's only suitable for hanging your clothes on.

Beyond this waits the Admissions Room to U.N.C.L.E. Headquarters' New York command center. A pretty receptionist is obligatory, of course, and no one— least of all the vaguely lecherous Napoleon— ever seems to mind that one bit. A large television monitor kept a close eye on the shop outside (hidden in Del Floria's "broken" television). A bank of alarm controls, lists of official U.N.C.L.E. personnel, an intercom and the all-important badges were crucial components here. The receptionist's fingers were coated with a special chemical which activated the badges (as the THRUSH agents who raided HQ in

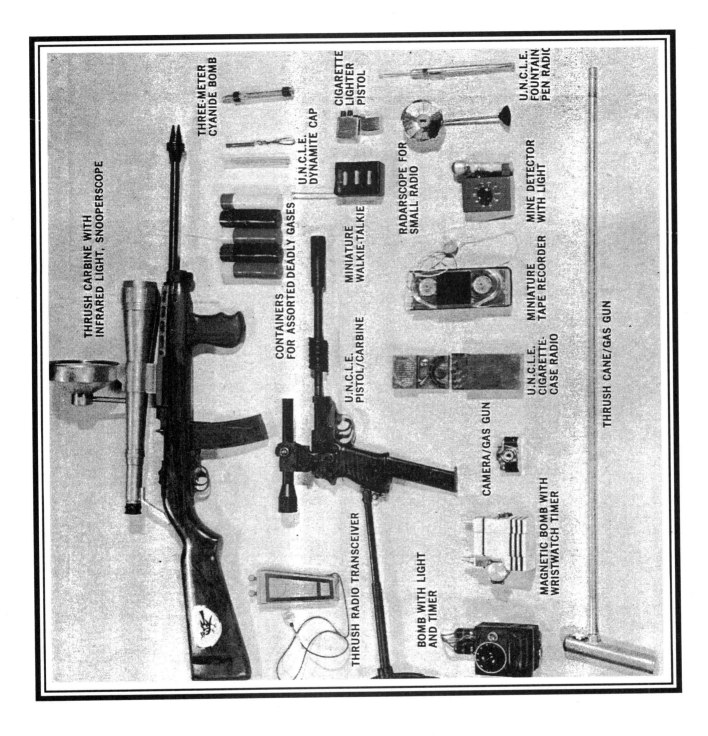

THRUSH CARBINE WITH INFRARED LIGHT, SNOOPERSCOPE

THREE-METER CYANIDE BOMB

CIGARETTE LIGHTER PISTOL

U.N.C.L.E. DYNAMITE CAP

U.N.C.L.E. FOUNTAIN PEN RADIO

CONTAINERS FOR ASSORTED DEADLY GASES

MINIATURE WALKIE-TALKIE

RADARSCOPE FOR SMALL RADIO

MINE DETECTOR WITH LIGHT

U.N.C.L.E. PISTOL/CARBINE

MINIATURE TAPE RECORDER

U.N.C.L.E. CIGARETTE CASE RADIO

THRUSH RADIO TRANSCEIVER

CAMERA/GAS GUN

MAGNETIC BOMB WITH WRISTWATCH TIMER

THRUSH CANE/GAS GUN

BOMB WITH LIGHT AND TIMER

"The Vulcan Affair" learned the hard way). Otherwise, the badges will trigger a special chemical alarm if they are taken beyond the reception area. These triangular badges come in four colors. Visitors and secretaries wear green. Red badges only allow access to the routine operations area, the two floors known as Sub and Ground.

Access to Level One and all lower levels can only be obtained with a yellow badge. White allows access to all levels; these were changed to yellow when the series went to color. The badges also triggered the various electronic doors that led one deeper into U.N.C.L.E. Headquarters. Waverly's badge bore the number 1; Illya Kuryakin was Number 2, and Napoleon Solo, despite ranking higher than Illya, was Number 11. The accepted explanation involves the first day of shooting: Will Kuluva (as Mr. Allison) chose a badge numbered one, and Robert Vaughn, thinking in terms of Roman numerals, took 11 thinking it was two. David McCallum wound up with Arabic numeral 2 by default. But is this true? In the movie version of the pilot, Will Kuluva never wears a badge.

INSIDE HEADQUARTERS

The corridor after Admissions is an impressive set: just over fifty-nine feet in length, and eight feet wide, it lends an impressive air of importance to the last leg of Illya and Solo's daily commute. In the first seven episodes, their progress was detailed in the opening credits, and a narrator explained the basic set-up: this sequence was destined to be parodied in the opening sequence of the GET SMART series.

After the hallway, they reach a security post and pass through more sliding doors. This octagonal room was also the same set that served, redressed of course, as Waverly's office. (Napoleon's apartment was a redress of the Admissions Room set, which appeared in other guises as well: a radar post and an interrogation chamber.)

As THRUSH discovered in "The Vulcan File," intruders will trigger an elaborate security system: locking doors, sliding dividers, and flashing lights would trap the intruder and alert U.N.C.L.E. security.

There were other ways in to U.N.C.L.E. HQ, but they were never shown: a tunnel to the

East River, and in the locker rooms of the garage attached to the outside of the U.N.C.L.E. complex. On the roof was a helicopter landing pad, a laser defense apparatus and a secret communications antenna array hidden inside a neon sign (never seen on the show, but included in Sam Rolfe's detailed background notes).

ARMAMENTS

The U.N.C.L.E. Special, that impressive piece of personal artillery which got our heroes Solo and Illya out of so many jams, was designed by Bob Murdock, Rudy Butler, Arnold Goode and Manuel Zamora, prop men at MGM Studios. This first U.N.C.L.E. Special was a 1934 model Mauser handgun, modified with a removable barrel that could be replaced with a barrel extension instead, and new grips. On the left side, a Bushnel "Phantom" scope could easily be mounted. This was a real gun, adapted to fire as a full automatic. After five or so episodes, the Mauser was replaced by the P-38, the most familiar of the U.N.C.L.E. guns. There were six real guns altered for this purpose, outfitted with grips like the ones utilized on the Mausers, but with a square insignia area for the agents' initials (always a priority in a secret organization!), solid aluminum grips that fit over the standard P-38 grip.

The same attachments, including the Bushnell scope, could be used with the new U.N.C.L.E. P-38s, as well as some new ones. There were only attachments for two of the six guns. Again, the guns were adapted for full automatic use. An extended magazine held sixteen rounds, but the guns would jam after a dozen shots were fired. Besides, when the carbine barrel was threaded onto the gun, it was impossible to fire live ammunition anyway. This was not particularly important since this was a television show. But in real life, U.N.C.L.E. agents would have been in pretty serious trouble if they had to rely on these cool-looking but ineffective weapons.

Generally, the guns were supposedly used to fire tranquilizer bullets, or sleep darts, largely created through the use of post-production sound effects. Rubber models were used for scenes involving water or any risk to the valuable props, as well as for hitting people over the head— the Screen Actors' Guild has strict regulations about that sort of thing! The female U.N.C.L.E.

agents in the New York Headquarters, on the other hand, generally had to content themselves with black plastic water pistols, courtesy of the Eldon company. Occasionally one of them would get a real prop, for realism's sake, but since these guns remained in their holsters anyway, the toys worked just fine.

TECH TOYS FOR SPIES

In the tradition of Ian Fleming's Q Division, THE MAN FROM U.N.C.L.E. saw fit to provide its characters with a wide variety of clever devices. Among these were a number of communications devices called, of all things, communicators. The first one designed took the form of a Marlboro cigarette box that flipped open and contained buttons and dials. But the notion of giving Marlboro a free advertisement every episode gave NBC cold feet, even in that age when cigarettes were still advertised on television. After all, the replacement communicator was still based on the same idea: a cigarette case. Inside, realistic cigarettes (always five!) revealed a speaker/microphone grid, dials, buttons, et cetera. This

also involved an alligator clip (for antenna purposes) and a grounding wire. The U.N.C.L.E. parabolic mike (with reflector and suction cup) could be used with this device as well.

In the second season opener "The Alexander The Greater Affair," a new communicator was introduced: the pen communicator. Even more compact than the cigarette case version, all you had to do was make sure that nobody walked away with your pen, and you could contact U.N.C.L.E. any time, anywhere. Actually, this one was more a short-range device to allow agents to communicate in the field. U.N.C.L.E. agents always seemed to use Channel D— there were apparently other channels but they never were used on the show. And on THE GIRL FROM U.N.C.L.E., the communicator pens had the female agents' names engraved on them. (Again— an odd touch for a top secret organization!)

The briefcase communicator contained a good deal more hi-fi equipment, but wasn't that concealable. You needed an excuse to be carrying a briefcase into THRUSH headquarters for it to be effective. A more compact cigarette case communicator also came into play later in the series run.

DRIVING IN STYLE

Hot rod custom cars were another big thing in the sixties, and everybody who was anybody in popular culture had some sort of gimmick vehicle. Again, it may have been James Bond with his Aston-Martin who kicked the movie/TV car craze off. The Batmobile (from that troublesome show over on CBS!) really threw this situation into high gear. Felton and his production team got to thinking— why didn't the men from U.N.C.L.E. have a souped up, spiffy, super-stylish car like every other hero in town? The man to turn to as the solution to this problem was custom auto wizard Gene Winfield, who is remembered not only for the U.N.C.L.E. car but also for the Galileo shuttlecraft on STAR TREK and Maxwell Smart's car on GET SMART.

The original plan for U.N.C.L.E. was to adapt the new Dodge Charger to the needs of a secret agent. But the auto company expressed reservations about linking their car with a violent TV show, and Winfield was obliged to scrap his designs at the last moment. Also, NBC was once again reluctant to grant free advertising with this large example of product placement. Luckily, he had a car of his own design, the Piranha, on hand to take the Charger's place.

With its gull-wing doors and sleek design, it looked like a car a high tech spy might drive— as long as he didn't mind telling the world that he was a high-tech spy. In fact, even though this is a famous car, it was only used in five episodes of THE MAN FROM U.N.C.L.E., and once on the spin-off series THE GIRL FROM U.N.C.L.E.. The reason: the stars, especially Robert Vaughn, didn't like it. It was awkward to get in and out of. The electrical system didn't work very well. It looked a bit too loud to be a spy's car. The list goes on.

The car was "armed" with non-functional machine guns that were concealed in the body, a "bullet screen," a braking parachute, and a host of very cool gadgets and weapons. Despite its limited use, it is widely remembered as a key feature of THE MAN FROM U.N.C.L.E..

Chapter Eleven

THE CAR FROM U.N.C.L.E.

Originally constructed by A.M.T.'s Speed & Custom Division, under the supervision of Gene Winfield, the MAN FROM U.N.C.L.E. car is a one of a kind vehicle based on a car which Winfield had designed and built himself for displaying in car shows. He had one of those special cars redone for the series, but the U.N.C.L.E. car started out being a different vehicle altogether. "I had made some contacts in the film business when I was still in Modesto and had landed the contract to build a car for the U.N.C.L.E. series," Winfield recalled. "This original version was going to be based on the Dodge Challenger, a car which was just hitting the market that year. The producers liked that car because it had such a distinctive design and the customizing and altering of it into a spy car wouldn't have changed the outward appearance much at all.

"Our designs for the Challenger conversion had been approved by the producers and one of the cars had already been delivered to me from Dodge when the network [NBC] put the kibosh on the idea. It seems that with all the free advertising the car would receive by being in the series, Dodge might decide to curtail what would otherwise by a multi-million dollar advertising campaign. We were all ready to do that car. We even had all of the accessories we needed from Dodge."

After Gene Winfield relocated his business from Modesto to Arizona, he approached A.M.T. and the producers of U.N.C.L.E. with an alternate idea for the car. "This was a year after the cancellation of the Dodge Challenger concept, and this time I suggested the U.N.C.L.E. car be based on the Piranha, a limited production car which I had designed. Since this car was unconnected with any major automobile manufacturer, and didn't look like anything Detroit was producing then, they decided to go for it."

NBC was also enticed by the fact that the U.N.C.L.E. car would be provided to the series for free as part of the deal with A.M.T. for the model kit license. A.M.T. spent between 30 and 40 thousand dollars constructing the U.N.C.L.E. car but they felt it was worth it since its existence on the show was free advertising for the model kit.

SPECIAL FEATURES

The U.N.C.L.E. car's exterior design was essentially the Piranha with some subtle changes, primarily on the rear end. The car also had a Corvair engine mounted in the rear. The frame of the U.N.C.L.E. car is made from Fiberglas with a steel cage frame housing the front and rear suspension. The body (except for the doors, trunk and hood) was a solid piece of Cycolac, a thermoplastic manufactured by the Marbon Chemical Company.

The car included such unique features as a grille which could revolve to reveal twin (operational)

flame-throwers. The mock laser beams built into the front and rear were never operational, nor were the rocket-launchers built into the gull-wing doors. Although not used on the show, a braking parachute was successfully tested on the car.

Inside the car, the dash panel revolved to reveal a video center with a digital computer, radar screen and infrared television system. "We installed genuine wood grain, not a cheap imitation finish," Gene explained. "We built the car to be absolutely real and functional. Even the propellers, which could be lowered from the rear, were operational. The car wasn't amphibious, although with just a little extra work we could have made it capable of that, if they'd wanted it."

Bob Short with restored U.N.C.L.E. car.

The car was also built with a specially designed independent electronic system so that any problems could be quickly traced. But after U.N.C.L.E. was canceled the car was sold and fell into a sad state of disrepair.

THE RETURN

In 1981 special effects technician Bob Short (who has worked on such films as STAR TREK—THE MOTION PICTURE, E.T., SPLASH and BEETLEJUICE, and also as a consultant on RETURN OF THE MAN FROM U.N.C.L.E.) bought the car and began six months of restoration work.

Armed with the original wiring diagram used by Gene Winfield some fifteen years before, Bob was able to accurately reconnect all of the car's special electrical features. The result was that the U.N.C.L.E. car not only looks as good as new but it runs as good too.

Seeing the U.N.C.L.E. car up close allows for some interesting observations. For instance, because of the way the gull-wing doors were designed, one had to climb over the side of the car to get in. It's a snug fit in the bucket seats and there was no way that the actors could just run up to the car and jump in the way that they could with any ordinary car. In the show you'd see Solo and Kuryakin running to the car and then the scene would cut to them already inside the car. Getting in and was not graceful.

The car is sleek and fun to ride around in and was clearly U.N.C.L.E.'s answer to James Bond's gadget equipped Aston Martin DB5. A scripted flashback scene in the 1983 TV movie THE RETURN OF THE MAN FROM THE U.N.C.L.E. would have briefly shown the U.N.C.L.E. car, but when the scene was cut from the shooting schedule, any chance of the car being seen in THE FIFTEEN YEARS LATER AFFAIR went along with it.

Chapter Twelve

THE GIRL FROM U.N.C.L.E.

During that meeting which Norman Felton had with Ian Fleming, the creator of James Bond came up with another character name which was pure Fleming—April Dancer. This idea lay dormant until 1965 when NBC came to Felton with the idea of coming up with an U.N.C.L.E. spin-off.

Initially Felton had forgotten the name April Dancer. When the writer, Martha Wilkerson, approached to develop the spin-off character, she suggested Cookie Fortune as the name of the female U.N.C.L.E. agent. A memo Norman Felton sent to producer David Victor on August 23, 1965 stated: "What we need to do is use a woman agent but to (do) a series which has basically the same flavor as our present Man From U.N.C.L.E. show, using the same U.N.C.L.E. headquarters and set-up. In this way, we make the best use of the so-called U.N.C.L.E. mystique."

The series was initially thought to be called THE LADY FROM U.N.C.L.E. and was at first looked at as being only a half-hour show. With a female lead they didn't think it could sustain itself as a one-hour action show. During development stages it was decided to give "Cookie Fortune" a partner. That partner would be a man, named Mark Slate. They decided to make Slate an older, wiser agent who could give advice to the new recruit.

Mary Ann Mobley, a former Miss America, was chosen to play Miss Fortune. Norman Fell was Mark Slate. On November 8,1965 producer Felton wrote to NBC president Grant Tinker suggesting that they just do two hours each week under the U.N.C.L.E. heading: "It would also follow that we would have episodes on either hour with Solo, Illya, Miss Fortune and Mark appearing in any combination that seemed best." But NBC didn't care for this idea, preferring that THE GIRL FROM U.N.C.L.E. be a separate series entirely. Also in November, the

name Cookie Fortune was dropped and replaced with April Dancer. Felton told Tinker, "reading over Ian Fleming's notes I recalled, and found in his own handwriting, the name of 'April Dancer' as a suggestion for a girl. It seemed a good idea to use it as it has a nice flair to it."

INTRODUCING: APRIL DANCER

"The Moonglow Affair," written by Martha Wilkerson, aired February 25, 1966 and introduced April Dancer, played by Mary Ann Mobley, and Mark Slate played by Norman Felton. Although NBC ordered that a series go into production based on that episode, they wanted both Mary Ann Mobley and Norman Fell replaced. In fact they even suggested Stefanie Powers as the new GIRL FROM U.N.C.L.E. Norman Felton resisted the casting changes but in March 1966 had no choice but to give in if the series was going to be accepted by NBC.

Stefanie Powers (real name Stefanie Zofja Federkievicz) had just finished her eleventh film, a remake of STAGE-COACH, and was a popular young actress. Mary Ann Mobley was just starting out

and her career never did take off. Powers went on after GIRL FROM U.N.C.L.E. to co-star in the very successful '70s series HART TO HART and was dating William Holden at the time of his tragic death. After being out of the spotlight for some time, Stefanie Powers reteamed with Robert Wagner on the TV movie THE RETURN OF HART TO HART which aired Nov. 5, 1993.

Noel Harrison, the son of actor Rex Harrison, was cast as Mark Slate. This completely changed the dynamics of the show as Slate was no longer an old-timer showing the young new agent the ropes. Harrison and Powers were clearly contemporaries, just like Vaughn and McCallum. Mark Slate was now an agent out of the British branch of U.N.C.L.E. working in America. Harrison was also a pop singer who had recorded the theme from THE THOMAS CROWN AFFAIR as well as other successful pop melodies.

THE SILLY SEASON

THE GIRL FROM U.N.C.L.E. went into production in May 1966 with "The Horns of the Dilemma Affair." The show was produced by Douglas Benton, with executive producer David Victor. The show quickly started going over budget due to expensive guest-stars and large, silly sets such as a giant toaster. The only season (a full year) of THE GIRL FROM U.N.C.L.E. paralleled the disastrous third season of THE MAN FROM U.N.C.L.E. Just as it is in 1993, in 1966 television was being assailed from all sides for presenting gratuitous violence. As a result the show changed its focus to up the humor count and made the stories too outrageous to offend anyone—except for U.N.C.L.E. fans who couldn't believe what they were seeing.

Norman Felton criticized Douglas Benton for going over budget and making THE GIRL FROM U.N.C.L.E. too silly when, frankly, it had more class and style than the dreary third season of THE MAN FROM U.N.C.L.E. did.

THE GIRL FROM U.N.C.L.E. came across as being more in the tradition of THE AVENGERS and was more successful at pulling off its brand of silliness than Norman Felton was with THE MAN FROM U.N.C.L.E., whose third season was just plain awful. One of the more inspired episodes of GIRL guest-starred Boris Karloff in drag as "Mother Muffin," and it was amusing. GIRL FROM U.N.C.L.E. was definitely different from MAN FROM U.N.C.L.E. whereas the MAN FROM U.N.C.L.E. that year came across as a poor imitation of what was being done over on GIRL FROM U.N.C.L.E.

THE GIRL FROM U.N.C.L.E. was canceled after one year and THE MAN FROM U.N.C.L.E. barely survived into its fourth season.

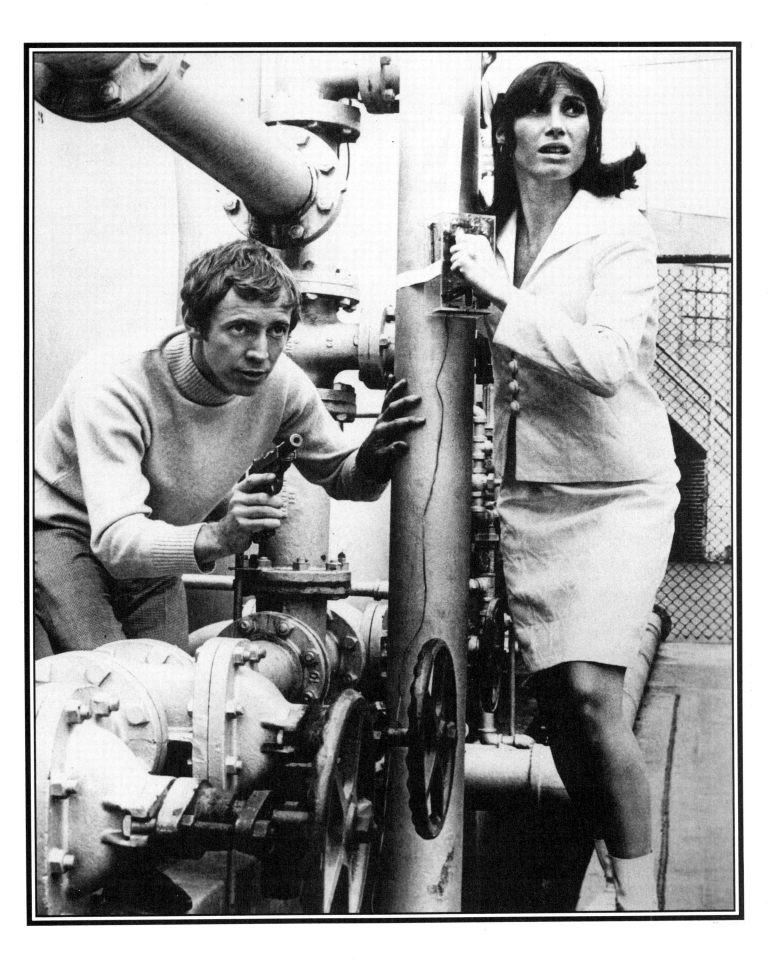

The following is the original text of the MGM promotional booklet for THE GIRL FROM U.N.C.L.E. prepared after the pilot was shot—but before the series went into production. The two leads were subsequently recast with Stefanie Powers replacing Mary Ann Mobley and Noel Harrison replacing Norman Fell, but this promotional item attempted to sell NBC on the original GIRL FROM U.N.C.L.E. cast, which the network rejected. The original style of the booklet, including the frequent use of "all caps" in the typeface has been retained as much as possible.

THE GIRL FROM U.N.C.L.E.

FLASH!

FROM U.N.C.L.E. HEADQUARTERS

NEW AGENT APRIL DANCER HAS JOINED U.N.C.L.E.

INCREASED ACTIVITY BY THRUSH WITH DEADLY EFFECT IN ALL CORNERS OF THE WORLD HAS MADE IT HIGHLY ADVISABLE TO HAVE THE GIRL FROM U.N.C.L.E. AVAILABLE FOR SEPARATE COUNTER MOVES FROM THOSE EMPLOYED BY THE MAN FROM U.N.C.L.E. MARK SLATE, A VETERAN AGENT OF VAST EXPERIENCE WITH U.N.C.L.E., HAS BEEN ASSIGNED TO WORK CLOSELY WITH HER.

ATTENTION NAPOLEON SOLO AND ILLYA KURYAKIN:

IT DOUBTLESS WILL NOT ESCAPE YOUR NOTICE THAT SHE IS THE SWINGINGEST, COOLEST AGENT EVER TO TOTE AN U.N.C.L.E. SPECIAL. THERE'S SOMETHING SPECIAL ABOUT THE GIRL FROM U.N.C.L.E., TOO.

DON'T LET HER SEX AND HER BEAUTY MISLEAD YOU. YOU WILL DISCOVER THAT SHE IS FIVE FEET, FIVE INCHES AND 108 POUNDS OF RAVEN-HAIRED DANGER.

(signed)
MR. WAVERLY

Section 1, No. 1

METRO-GOLDWYN-MAYER
TELEVISION
Presents
An Arena Production
"THE GIRL FROM U. N. C. L. E."
Starring
Mary Ann Mobley
Norman Fell
C-Starring
Leo G. Carroll
Executive Producer: Norman Felton
Supervising Producer: David Victor
Pilot Episode Written by Dean Hargrove
In Color, for the 1966-67 Season on the NBC Television Network

DURING THE PAST TWO SEASONS, NAPOLEON SOLO, ILLYA KURYAKIN AND MR. WAVERLY HAVE PARLAYED THEIR MAD-CAP, TONGUE-IN-CHEEK ADVENTURES INTO TELEVISION'S MOST SPECTACULAR HIT.

AND NOW COMES "THE GIRL FROM U.N.C.L.E.", BEARING THE SAME DISTINCTIVE STAMP OF UNIQUE, 'WAY-OUT DERRING-DO, THE SAME PROMISE OF SUPER-EXCITEMENT AND SUPERB FUN. PLUS, ITS OWN INDIVIDUAL ASSET — GLAMOROUS, VIVACIOUS APRIL DANCER — U.N.C.L.E. AGENT BEYOND COMPARE.

APRIL — AND MARK SLATE — FORM A NEW TEAM OF U.N.C.L.E. AGENTS TO DO BATTLE WITH THRUSH. IT'S A SPARKLING, DIFFERENT TEAM.

As Mark Slate says: "Things just aren't the same around U.N.C.L.E. A 17-year-old agent, and a girl at that!"

It doesn't matter that she's really 24. Not to Mark, who carefully avoids pointing out what April puts into words: "I thought agents over 40 weren't allowed assignments in the field."

Nevertheless, and though he sometimes may feel like he's playing nursemaid, Mark Slate likes this girl. As Mr. Waverly decides: "They work well together."

APRIL DANCER . . .

She's a lovely girl of 24, a college graduate (psychology, languages), blessed with a quick wit, intuition, and deadly feminine charm, which she doesn't hesitate to use to full advantage when threatened by THRUSH, or any evil.

April has almost completed her U.N.C.L.E. training in Section 2 (Enforcement) when the confident Mr. Waverly throws her into the clutches of THRUSH.

From her bottomless handbag (as with most women), April can come up with any of her specially designed exotic weaponry.

But her biggest weapon is her good, old-fashioned, devastating sex appeal!

Her private life?

Well, THAT'S too private to even discuss. . .

Played by. . . . MARY ANN MOBLEY . . .

Mary Ann Mobley is the only "Miss America" to have achieved the ultimate goal of nearly every contestant. . . a successful career in motion pictures, television and the legitimate stage.

A native of Mississippi, she broke into Broadway in "No Where to Go But Up", for producer Kermit Bloomgarten. She then went into summer stock with Betty Grable and Dan Dailey in "Guys And Dolls" at Melodyland, which led to her first starring film, "Girl Happy", opposite Elvis Presley. She recently starred with Jerry Lewis in "Three On A Couch".

AND THEN THERE'S . . . . MARK SLATE

A quiet-spoken bachelor, Slate is a rarity in U.N.C.L.E. He has a secret, which if discovered, could retire him from active spy-chasing — he's "somewhere around" 40, the mandatory age at which all U.N.C.L.E. agents are retired from the field.

Mr. Waverly is quite aware of Slate's secret, but since he happens to be Waverly's finest trainer of U.N.C.L.E. agents (Solo and Illya are two of his prize graduates), the old chief merely ignores the point.

Waverly's respect for Slate is so great that he teams the 15-year veteran with April in order to keep a protective eye on the pretty U.N.C.L.E. fledgling as she plunges into death-defying adventure.

PLAYED BY . . . . NORMAN FELL

A veteran performer of feature pictures, the Broadway stage and television, Fell previously was a continuing star in TV's "87th Precinct".

His more than 100 TV roles have included guest star parts in "Perry Mason", "The Untouchables", "The Eleventh Hour", "Dr. Kildare" and "The Fugitive".

Motion pictures in which he has played leading roles have included "Pork Chop Hill," "Inherit The Wind", "It's A Mad, Mad, Mad, Mad World" and "Ocean's 11".

AND, OF COURSE, THERE'S . . . . MR. WAVERLY

Mr. Waverly, one of the men at the peak of U.N.C.L.E.'s organizational structure, has a poor memory when it comes to names and other trivia. So he talks around them and other unimportant details. Though he may forget the names of the operatives facing him, Waverly nonetheless fully is aware of the dangers involved in the situations into which he is placing U.N.C.L.E.'s men.

A tweedy man, he stands out in stark contrast to the sleek, twentieth-century organization of which he is a guiding force. The issue of his life or death leaves him unmoved; a duel, once ended, is done with, and nothing to sit around and talk about.

Waverly has a habit of turning up in odd, out-of-the-way places, if for no other reason than to spot-check April and Slate.

PLAYED BY . . . . LEO G. CARROLL

The veteran actor made his professional stage debut in 1911 in "The Prisoner of Zenda" and since has appeared on the London and Broadway stage as well as in stock, in more than 50 plays.

He has starred in more than 30 films, including "Rebecca", "Wuthering Heights", "The Bad and The Beautiful" and "The Prize". Mr. Carroll also has guest starred on "Hazel", "Kraft Theatre", "Thriller" and dozens of other top TV shows and became identified as "Topper" during five years in that hit series before donning the tweeds of Alexander Waverly in "U.N.C.L.E.".

PLUS THOSE OTHER GOOD AGENTS OF. . . . . . U.N.C.L.E.

April Dancer and Mark Slate, as well as Solo, Illya, Mr. Waverly and countless other colorful U.N.C.L.E. agents, operate out of a row of buildings in New York's East Fifties.

The entrance is masked by Del Floria's, an ancient, pants-pressing establishment behind which is a large building, three floors of a modern, complex office structure. Through its maze of corridors and suites pass. . . sometimes rush. . . U.N.C.L.E. agents of many races, creeds and national origins.

U.N.C.L.E. headquarters, with its complex masses of modern technological equipment, is the heart, brain and body of the organization. There, U.N.C.L.E. agents become concerned with anything and everything that effects the welfare of people or countries anywhere in the world.

AND THOSE DASTARDLY AGENTS FROM. . . . . . . THRUSH

Remember those nasty villains from THRUSH. . . Dr. Dabree (and her brain-killing machine), Professor Amdeus (who tried to revive the "pickled" body of a long-dead dictator), Angelique (and her poisonous spider), and all the others?

THRUSH. . . let U.N.C.L.E. be warned. . . has more such ingenious, highly scientific cut-throats . . . equally evil. . . equally menacing to all good people. . . and to THE GIRL FROM U.N.C.L.E.

THRUSH agents are an international group for hire. . . cunning, ruthless and well-heeled both in cash and in manpower. They have one purpose . . . to dominate the earth.

THRUSH's head may be a man. . . or a woman. . . or even a computer. It is never seen, but its presence is always felt.

U.N.C.L.E. means many things to many people. . .

ADVENTURE, FUN, GLAMOUR, THE BIZARRE. . . As millions of viewers have discovered each week, the "U.N.C.L.E." hour is definitely NOT the time to raid the ice box. If you turn around, you'll miss something.

The same is true of THE GIRL FROM U.N.C.L.E. Besides, who could turn his back on a dish like that?

"THEY'RE COOL, THEY'RE HIP, THEY'RE GEAR. IF THEY HAD A LITTLE LESS TALENT, THEY MIGHT EVEN BE CAMP.

THEY'RE THE TEENAGERS' LATEST DREAM-BOATS, THE ESCAPISTS' GEMINI TWINS ORBITING BY ONCE A WEEK. . . THEY'RE. . . 'THE MEN FROM U.N.C.L.E.' "

Newsweek Magazine

E V E R Y B O D Y . . . .

But E V E R Y B O D Y

Is talking about "U.N.C.L.E."

LIFE MAGAZINE

"My instinct when I first saw U.N.C.L.E. — I recall with a twinge of conscience — was to keep the discovery to myself as I would the discovery of a superb but inexpensive restaurant. But I didn't. And I'm glad. Lord knows who the guy I introduced to U.N.C.L.E. went and told. But I don't think I ever helped save a better show."

TIME MAGAZINE

"THE MAN FROM U.N.C.L.E. is the most popular new hero on the television scene. . . "

McCALL'S MAGAZINE

"THE MAN FROM U.N.C.L.E. is one of the few shows that last year climbed up from nowhere to the top ten, that gradually built its own semisatirical style of derring-do."

PRAVDA HATES U.N.C.L.E. . . . .

Pravda's Man from U.N.C.L.E. Yuri Zhukov
Translated from PRAVDA, Moscow

Television viewers in the U.S. have settled into a steady diet of "The Man from U.N.C.L.E.," the hyperbolic spy serial about the derring-do of a new breed of international secret agents, among them, a fearless but rather cosmopolitan Russian named Illya Kuryakin. Predictably, Pravda doesn't like Illya. Its comment:

AMERICAN television, and later the Metro-Goldwyn-Mayer Film Corporation, have created a film series devoted to a certain international organization which, to the author's mind, would not be a bad substitute for the present U.N. It is called U.N.C.L.E., or United Network Command for Law and Enforcement.

The U.N.C.L.E. staff is made up of persons of various nationalities "experienced in business affairs and intelligence" whose set task is the "defense of the interests and well-being of the peoples and nations the world over against subversive (read "democratic") forces. At the head of this "organization" are five men of various nationalities, including a certain scoundrel of Russian descent named "Illya Kuryakin, who, like many other U.N.C.L.E. agents, used to work behind the Iron Curtain." He, like James Bond, "works like a machine, without reasoning, and precisely executes the orders of Mr. Efficiency."

In striving to command the attention of reader and viewer, the preachers of "the right to kill" will stop at nothing. They deliberately corrupt young people, using stronger and stronger doses of bloodthirtiness, eroticism and violence. . .

THE UNITED NATIONS IS A BIT PERPLEXED OVER "U.N.C.L.E." CONFUSED TV VIEWERS

U.N. Gets Stream of U.N.C.L.E. Applicants

UNITED NATIONS, N.Y.(AP) — American television viewers are flooding the United Nations with inquiries about U.N.C.L.E. They think it's the espionage arm of the United Nations, and they want to enlist.

In recent months, the United Nations' General Services division has been deluged with letters and telephone calls from fans of the NBC program The Man from U.N.C.L.E.

"It's the 'U.N.' in the title that gets them," said Maurice Liu, director of the division. "And when they hear that bit of hokum that the show would not have been possible without the help of U.N.C.L.E., they are sure we are tied up with it."

Napoleon Solo and Illya Kuryakin work for the U.N. Command for Law and Enforcement, but the 'U.N.' stands for United Network, not United Nations.

"Most of the applications come from teenagers," said Liu, "but there are some adults, too, and they are the hardest to convince that we are not running a spy ring.

"One guy was so intent on becoming a secret agent that we finally suggested that he get in touch with Interpol (the International Police Organization). I don't know what they told him."

The queries come in from all over the country.

One youthful applicant from Silver City, N.C. asked if he could join the spy ranks before he was 21. He wanted to know the location of the U.N.C.L.E. branch nearest his hometown.

An enterprising youth from Brooklyn wrote directly to U Thant, asking whether the secretary-general minded if he started his own U.N.C.L.E. branch. He assured Thant that he was not trying to undercut the organization but would "take orders from the head."

And already the talk has begun. . .

      about. . .

"THE GIRL FROM U.N.C.L.E."

YES. . . THE GIRL FROM U.N.C.L.E. HAS EVERYTHING GOING FOR HER.

THE TEEN-AGERS AND THE PRE-TEENS. . . THE YOUNG ADULTS AND THE OLDER ADULTS.

HUNDREDS OF THOUSANDS OF CARD-HOLDING U.N.C.L.E. AGENTS IN VIRTUALLY EVERY U.S. CITY.

U.N.C.L.E. FAN CLUBS IN COLLEGES AND HIGH SCHOOLS. . . IN BIG BUSINESS OFFICES AND SMALL SOCIAL GROUPS. . . IN ALMOST ANY NEIGHBORHOOD ALMOST ANYWHERE.

THE SAME U.N.C.L.E. ORGANIZATION THAT HAS BUILT THE MAN FROM U.N.C.L.E. INTO AN UNPARALLELED SUCCESS

STORY. . . THAT HAS WON HONORS AND AWARDS RIGHT AND LEFT. . . AND THAT HAS CAUSED MORE. . .

TALK. . . TALK. . . TALK. . . IN THE PRESS, THE INDUSTRY AND AMONG VIEWERS. . . THAN HAS BEEN HEARD IN RECENT TELEVISION HISTORY.

THE PILOT EPISODE

Cast

April Dancer	MARY ANN MOBLEY
Mark Slate	NORMAN FELL
Napoleon Solo	ROBERT VAUGHN
Illya Kuryakin	DAVID McCALLUM
Alexander Waverly	LEO G. CARROLL
Arthur Gordon	KEVIN McCARTHY
Jean	Mary Carver
Andy Watson	Woodrow Parfrey
Marylin	Victoria Carroll
Carl	Rick Traeger
Dr. Swift	Byron Morrow
Dr. Moderna	R. Wayland Williams
Dr. Faust	Noel DeSouza
Farmer	Andy Albin
Sally	Kay Michaels

The Credits
Executive Producer, Norman Felton
Produced by David Victor
Directed by Joseph Sargent
Written by Dean Hargrove
Director of Photography, Fred Koenekamp

SYNOPSIS OF THE PILOT

When U.N.C.L.E. discovers a world-wide THRUSH plot to sabotage both the U.S. and Russian moon expeditions, Alexander

Waverly (Number 1, Section 1) immediately sends Solo and Illya to prevent the disaster.

They discover that Caresse, a debonair THRUSH chieftain, has been operating behind the cover of a legitimate cosmetic firm, from which THRUSH's space plans emanate.

The pair are trapped and rendered helpless by Caresse's deadly Quartzite Radiation projector, which destroys their equilibrium and promises certain death within 48 hours if the radiation is not reversed.

Waverly, with his two top U.N.C.L.E. agents hopelessly out of circulation, must call on April Dancer, a pretty and intelligent, but inexperienced agent trainee, and Mark Slate, a fortyish 15-year U.N.C.L.E. veteran and chief trainer of U.N.C.L.E. agents.

April joins the Caresse Company disguised as a fashion designer, and discovers THRUSH has its own space plans in work, including beating the rest of the world to the moon by irradiating the U.S. and Russian spaceman's food, causing their capsules to career out of control and crash.

As April pokes through secret files in the basement of the Caresse Building, she is discovered by one of THRUSH's chief scientists, who falls for her sexy wiles and spills the secret of the radiation machine. If reversed, it can return Illya and Solo to normal.

April, using her pen-communicator, radios Slate, telling him THRUSH is intending to dispose of Illya in a dump truck. While Slate rescues the dazed Illya, April suddenly finds herself the romantic object of Caresse, who picks her as "Miss Moonglow", the name of his new fluorescent lipstick, which glows in the dark.

Caresse's sister, highly suspicious and jealous of April's sudden importance, checks with THRUSH central.

When she tells her brother she has learned that April has U.N.C.L.E. connections, Caresse traps April in his library, spying her glowing lips in the darkness. She kisses him soundly before dashing up the stairs just as Caresse's sister enters. Seeing his lips now glowing, she empties her pistol into him and. . . scratch one THRUSH chieftain!

As April runs from the building, an army of U.N.C.L.E. agents descends, led by agent Slate. Waverly reassures them that Solo and Illya will recover completely, but that the team of April Dancer and Mark Slate will continue to work together in U.N.C.L.E.'s never-ending battle against THRUSH.

###

"THE GIRL FROM U. N. C. L. E. "

is filmed with all of the production values and creative talent of. . .

METRO-GOLDWYN-MAYER TELEVISION

and of

EXECUTIVE PRODUCER NORMAN FELTON AND ARENA PRO-
DUCTIONS, INC.

Norman Felton and his Arena Productions, joined MGM-TV
more than five years ago and produced "Dr. Kildare", an instant
popular hit, now in its fifth year. Other successes have followed
with Mr. Felton at the helm, including "The Eleventh Hour" and the
world-wide favorite, "The Man From U.N.C.L.E.", now in its second
year.

Felton, a veteran writer, director and producer in television, has
won a number of distinguished awards including two Christopher
Awards and an Emmy directing award. Prior to joining MGM-TV he
was with CBS-TV as executive producer and then as West Coast
Director of Programs. Previously he produced "Studio One" in New
York, directed "U.S. Steel Hour" for two seasons and also directed
"Hallmark Playhouse", "Alcoa Hour", "Goodyear Playhouse" and a
number of other distinguished dramatic programs.

The combined assets of Felton's production leadership and the
vast physical resources and creative talents offered by MGM, assure
the best in quality in every department.

SUPERVISING PRODUCER. . . AND PRODUCER OF THE PILOT
DAVID VICTOR. . .

Mr. Victor, Supervising Producer for Arena Productions and
known as one of TV's outstanding production and creative minds,
personally produced the pilot episode of "The Girl From
U.N.C.L.E.".

Long before he became producer of "The Man From U.N.C.L.E." as the series began its second season on NBC, Victor became established as a leading motion picture and television writer and winner of numerous awards. He produced the popular "Dr. Kildare" series for four years, then donned his cloak-and-dagger for U.N.C.L.E.

THE DIRECTOR OF THE PILOT. . . . . . JOSEPH SARGENT

One of the brightest young directors in television, Joseph Sargent has directed many episodes of "The Man From U.N.C.L.E.", and also "Dr. Kildare", "The Wackiest Ship In The Army", "Mr. Novak", "Ben Casey", "Daniel Boone", "Slattery's People" and other top network series.

THE WRITER OF THE PILOT. . . . . . . DEAN HARGROVE

Hargrove, a 27-year-old graduate of the University of Wichita and U.C.L.A., has become the backbone of the writing staff for "The Man From U.N.C.L.E.", with eight episodes to his credit. Prior to joining Arena Productions, he was a comedy writer for Bob Newhart. He also recently completed the screenplay of "Catch Me If You Can", to star Bob Hope.

Biography of

MARY ANN MOBLEY

Seldom has a new actress skyrocketed to Hollywood stardom with the speed of Mary Ann Mobley, who, as April Dancer in "The Girl From U.N.C.L.E.", promises to become video viewers' favorite feminine spy.

The former Miss America, who represents a combination of brains, beauty and talent, made her Hollywood motion picture debut in MGM's "Girl Happy", in which she was wooed by Elvis Presley. This was followed by a starring role in the light musical, "Get Yourself A College Girl", also for MGM, and the dramatic "Young Dillinger" for United Artists. She most recently starred with Elvis again in "Harum Scarum" and opposite Jerry Lewis in "Three On A Couch."

Born in Biloxi, Miss., on Feb. 17, Mary Ann was raised in the small town of Brandon, Miss., where her father, David Williams, is an attorney and her mother, Mrs. Mary Williams, operates an insurance agency in addition to her home-making activities. Mary Ann has a younger sister, Sandra.

Raised by the rather strict standards of a small rural community, Mary Ann remembers that she was not allowed to date until she was 16, had to be home by 10:30 p.m. "and was absolutely forbidden to go steady".

In her early years, Mary Ann developed as an equestrienne and still rides show horses and jumpers. She also studied singing and dancing, unaware that she was training for a future film career.

As a senior in Brandon High School, she won a four-year scholarship to the University of Mississippi. She had completed her junior year at Ol' Miss with an outstanding scholastic record when she agreed to enter the Miss Mississippi contest at the request of the Brandon Chamber of Commerce which, according to Mary Ann, "in such a small town didn't have many girls to choose from. They were stuck with me!"

Mary Ann's ambition was not necessarily to become Miss Mississippi or Miss America, but to at least share in some of the scholarship money which is distributed to contestants. With the money, she planned to study drama in New York.

But Mary Ann won the whole bundle, and as Miss America of 1959 spent a year touring the country. She then bade farewell to Ol' Miss and Chi Omega, and enrolled in a New York drama school with her $10,000 first prize money as a nest egg.

She commenced her career in New York television, then was signed for the ingenue lead in Kermit Bloomgarten's stage production of "Nowhere To Go But Up." However, there was another place to go — "down", Mary Ann recalls. The show closed after nine performances. Late in 1963, Mary Ann decided she was ready for Hollywood, and followed appearances in eastern stock companies starring in a West Coast presentation of "Guys and Dolls".

This opened the door for the dark-haired, dark-eyed beauty.

Biography of

NORMAN FELL

Norman Fell, a regular star as agent Mark Slate in "The Girl From U.N.C.L.E.", is a veteran of more than 150 television dramas, a number of feature motion pictures and the Broadway stage.

His films have included "It's A Mad, Mad, Mad, Mad World", "Pork Chop Hill" with Gregory Peck, "Ocean's 11" with Frank Sinatra, "Rat Race" with Debbie Reynolds and Tony Curtis, "Inherit the Wind", "P.T. 109" and most recently, for MGM, "Quick, Before It Melts".

In TV, he co-starred for a year as Detective Meyer in "87th Precinct" on NBC and has guest-starred in virtually every top series, including "The Defenders", "Chrysler Theatre", "Dick Powell Presents", "Ben Casey", "The Eleventh Hour", "Alfred Hitchcock" and "Kraft Suspense Theatre".

Fell was born in Philadelphia on March 24. He became interested in acting while serving as an Air Force aerial gunner in World War II. After the war, he enrolled in Temple University as a drama major, graduating in 1950. Another young actor, Marlon Brando, then suggested he study with Stella Adler in New York.

Two seasons in summer stock followed, then came his first TV shows in New York, and in 1956 he appeared on Broadway with Edward G. Robinson in "Middle of the Night". He later played Sammy's brother in NBC's two-part drama, "What Makes Sammy Run".

His first Hollywood film role came in 1958, in "Pork Chop Hill". His other pictures and his numerous TV appearances continued rapidly thereafter.

In the 1960's, people who watched television often liked to read about the fictional characters they watched on their favorite shows each week. In the case of THE MAN FROM U.N.C.L.E. books, the fans were provided with new adventures on a fairly regular basis, which continued even after the series was canceled, unlike the U.N.C.L.E. magazines which ceased when the TV show ended.

Chapter Thirteen

THE BOOKS FROM U.N.C.L.E.

Back in the sixties, television shows always inspired a variety of tie-ins, and one of the most popular of the time were paperback novels. Unlike today where a new TV series might inspire paperbacks based on scripts from aired episodes, in the sixties novels sold themselves by being original stories based on the series premise.

In the case of THE MAN FROM U.N.C.L.E., the book contract was licensed by Ace Books in the United States, and Souvenir Press/Four Square Books in Great Britain.

THE SHOW TAKES OFF

The first three novels published were THE THOUSAND COFFINS AFFAIR by Michael Avallone, THE DOOMSDAY AFFAIR by Harry Whittington and THE COPENHAGEN AFFAIR by John Oram. Although some sources claim that these were published concurrently, I remember only seeing THE THOUSAND COFFINS AFFAIR first followed by the other two novels some time later. The books themselves only bear a 1965 copyright with no publication date, although apparently U.N.C.L.E. #1 was published in December 1964, according to the author. There may well be a reason for the lack of publishing information in those books, though not a very good one.

In the '60s Ace Books was notorious for under reporting book sales for royalty purposes. Philip K. Dick's novel THE SOLAR LOTTERY went through numerous printings which were never reflected on his royalty statements, but he'd see them in stores and whenever Ave had a cover price increase, a new edition of SOLAR LOTTERY would follow. Leigh Brackett was told that two of her novels had low sales and each had different sales figures—even though they were both halves of

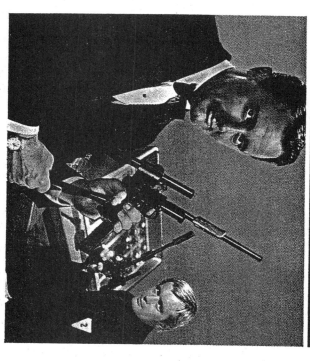

the same Ace double-novel! When the Science Fiction Writers of America forced an audit of Ace Books, writers started to suddenly get large royalty checks in the mail for books published years before.

Michael Avallone wasn't so fortunate since THE THOUSAND COFFINS AFFAIR wasn't science fiction nor did it come under the province of the audit instituted by the SFWA.

"Ace Books had no faith in the TV show," Avallone recalled, "was afraid it would flop and gave me a grand and a handshake on that one. The show soared, the world went U.N.C.L.E. crazy and my book stayed in print five years, sold in the millions and would end up in something like sixty foreign editions. There is no telling the royalty money I lost, but on the good side the book was always a great showcase for my talents, got me a lot of writing jobs and made me known abroad. To this day I meet people who still recall THE THOUSAND COFFINS AFFAIR as one of their memorable 'escape reading' experiences."

THE EARLY NOVELS

Due to lead time, the early U.N.C.L.E. novels were written before the first episode of the series ever aired and the authors had to use scripts and other background in crafting their stories. Basically they read like imitation James Bond since that was the standard of the day for espionage novels. THE DOOMSDAY AFFAIR by Harry Whittington, who would also write for the MAN FROM U.N.C.L.E. magazine a year later, was an interesting story which ended with Solo and Illya escaping from a car which had been boobytrapped with a heat bomb. The novel actually ended with the empty car exploding—end of story. Not exactly the relaxed kind of epilogue of an U.N.C.L.E. episode.

In 1965 the U.N.C.L.E. books being published in England and the United States stopped using the same numbering so that in England THE FINGER IN THE SKY AFFAIR by Peter Leslie was #5 even though it didn't appear in the United States until Ace U.N.C.L.E. #23 around 1971. Peter Leslie was a British writer who wrote several U.N.C.L.E. novels (as well as other TV spin-off books), but his stories tended to be a bit on the dry side and he didn't capture the characterization of Solo and Kuryakin as well as some of the other novelists did.

THE FINGER IN THE SKY AFFAIR bore a generic 1966 copyright and no publication date. It's uniquely impossible to tell exactly, or even approximately, when an U.N.C.L.E. novel was published by looking on the copyright page, a fact not true of virtually any other novel you might pick up in a used book store.

A NEW DIRECTION

Terry Carr, an editor an Ace, was dissatisfied with the U.N.C.L.E. novels the British writers were delivering and looking around for a writer to liven up the series he turned to David McDaniel, the then 22 year old author of the science fiction novel THE ARSENAL OF TIME. McDaniel, it turned out, was a fan of the new series and when approached to write an U.N.C.L.E. novel he enthusiastically crafted THE DAGGER AFFAIR, published as #4 in the Ace Books series. It captured the imagination, suspense, adventure and humor in the television series and those of us who were reading the then-new U.N.C.L.E. novels in the '60s immediately memorized this author's name and hoped he'd write more U.N.C.L.E. books.

McDaniel took it upon himself to take Thrush, which had always been spelled like the bird, and turn it into THRUSH, inventing for it the acronym the Technological Hierarchy for the Removal of Undesirables and the Subjugation of Humanity. McDaniel even decided that THRUSH had been founded in 1879 by one Professor Moriarty (the character invented by Sir Arthur Conan Doyle in the Sherlock Holmes story "The Final Problem"). Since MGM read and approved the book, this information became part of the official lore of U.N.C.L.E.

Along with U.N.C.L.E. fans Bob Short, Bill Mills and Don Simpson, McDaniel formed The Inner Circle II, a group of U.N.C.L.E. fans in Los Angeles. When the series was canceled they managed to acquire some of the original props from the series.

A REAL FAN

McDaniel wrote what are considered the best of the U.N.C.L.E. novels and those are #4: THE DAGGER AFFAIR (1965), #6: THE VAMPIRE AFFAIR (1966), #8: THE MONSTER WHEEL AFFAIR (1967), #13: THE RAINBOW AFFAIR (1967), #15: THE UTOPIA AFFAIR (1968), and #17: THE

HOLLOW CROWN AFFAIR (1969).

The U.N.C.L.E. novels by David McDaniel were fun and imaginative and filled with inside jokes. In THE DAGGER AFFAIR, the address for U.N.C.L.E. Los Angeles is the address of the MGM studios. The "DAGGER" of the title privately meant "Danger A-Go-Go and Electronic Revenge." In THE VAMPIRE AFFAIR, Forrest J Ackerman, the editor of FAMOUS MONSTERS OF FILMLAND, makes a cameo appearance when Solo and Illya save him from an angry mob who think that Forry is a vampire.

In THE MONSTER WHEEL AFFAIR, the first letter in each word in the chapter titles for the acronym "A A WYN IS A TIGHTWAD." A.A. Wyn was the publisher of Ace Books at the time. The funniest part is that you can see the acronym there on the contents page which lists every chapter title very neatly one above the other.

THE RAINBOW AFFAIR has allusions to such British detectives as Sherlock Holmes, John Steed and Miss Marple. In McDaniel's THE HOLLOW CROWN AFFAIR there are references made to the television show DARK SHADOWS, another of the author's favorite '60s TV shows.

U.N.C.L.E. VERSUS VAMPIRES

Bob Short, a founding member of the U.N.C.L.E. club the Inner Circle in the late '60s, recalled some memories of David and some of the things that McDaniel had told him about some of the novels David wrote.

"THE VAMPIRE AFFAIR was inspired by him watching 'The Birds And Bees Affair' in second season. There's a sequence at the beginning of the show where Solo and Illya go into one of the foreign headquarters and everyone's been killed from bee stings because THRUSH has let loose killer bees into the ventilating systems. As David was watching the beginning, and Solo and Illya go into this headquarters and discover all these dead U.N.C.L.E. agents (having been bitten by something), David turned to Joyce, his wife, and said, 'My God, they've been bitten by vampires!' Then, of course, the scene continued and it turned out to be killer bees.

"From that," Short explained, "he thought it would make for a great

U.N.C.L.E. story to actually put them up against vampires in Transylvania." At the time David McDaniel wrote THE VAMPIRE AFFAIR he had not yet seen "The Bat Cave Affair," although some might think that it was this latter episode with its ersatz Dracula which inspired David, but it was not.

FRIENDS AND CHARACTERS

"Most of the characters that appear in David's novels were based on real people that he knew," Bob explained. "There were a couple up in San Francisco, Mr. & Mrs. Dickensheet, who were the impetus for creating the Ward Baldwin character, one of the top THRUSH officials that continued to appear throughout the novels. To this day I never met them; I don't know who they were, but they were friends of David's from the San Francisco area, so he patterned Ward Baldwin and Irene after them."

Don Simpson, who was the fourth member of the new U.N.C.L.E. Inner Circle, and who was considered the "Q" of the group, was a science fiction fan who concocted odd gadgets such as special badges with secret compartments. He would make things like THRUSH communicators to inspire David while he was writing a novel. David put Don Simpson in the novels as the head of U.N.C.L.E. Scientific Branch, and so "Mr. Simpson" appears throughout David's novels.

"Other minor characters that would show up were people that were in the L.A. area of fandom," Bob recalled. "Forry (Ackerman) is in VAMPIRE AFFAIR because David knew Forry and he had taken from personal experiences of Forry's."

CREATIVE LEAPS

David was also interested in technological advances which were very much on the cutting edge for the time. "Actually much more so than the TV series was with doing a lot of theoretical research on stuff like the ball lightning gun that shows up, I think, in HOLLOW CROWN AFFAIR," Bob explained.

"He admitted that every once in awhile he'd just run out of ideas as to what to do with the stories and he'd slide something in. MONSTER WHEEL AFFAIR, he readily admitted, he did kind of as filler, and that if one really reads the novel there is no plot—just a bunch

of set pieces. He was just seeing how long he could string out a story without actually telling a story."

The only gun that David McDaniel had in the house was a Walther P-38 which he got because U.N.C.L.E. agents carried them on the shows. And he actually did, at times, wear the gun in a shoulder holster while writing the books. He did this to enhance the mood he wanted to achieve while writing.

"It was kind of fun because you'd walk in and David would be sitting there with a shoulder holster on, just typing away. If you took a photograph of him it would look staged," Bob stated.

"The reason why his novels are so much better than all the rest of them is just simply because he was really in to the characters and really understood what U.N.C.L.E. could be. And because he had that feeling for it, he was able to make those kind of creative leaps and create stuff for the U.N.C.L.E. universe that really seemed to fit.

"I think he was the only writer who was ever able to expand on what Sam Rolfe did and really create things that the fans came away believing was really part of the U.N.C.L.E. culture, as opposed to another writer trying to make up stuff and missing the boat."

THE FINAL AFFAIR

McDaniel also wrote an unpublished U.N.C.L.E. novel, THE FINAL AFFAIR, which would have tied things up since the series had been canceled by the time he wrote the book. But when he submitted the manuscript to Ace Books, they had already decided to cancel the U.N.C.L.E. paperback series. An attempt was made to issue a special limited edition of THE FINAL AFFAIR in the early '80s but MGM wouldn't grant a license. A bootlegged edition, published in a non-illustrated fanzine format, has been generally available in U.N.C.L.E. fandom for several years. Had it been published by Ace it would have been the official final U.N.C.L.E. novel in their series.

The only time it is known that David actually tried to write for the U.N.C.L.E. television series was around 1976 when MGM was thinking of reviving it and McDaniel presented them with THE FINAL AFFAIR as a possible storyline. But the studio decided that this wasn't what they were looking for, and then the revival plans drifted apart.

McDaniel was an unusual man. Although born David McDaniel on June 16, 1939, as a teenager he adopted the real-life pseudonym of "Ted Johnstone." In 1956 he joined the Los Angeles Fantasy Society as Ted Johnstone and wrote and edited fanzines under that name. His phone was even listed under Johnstone in the directory and when he attended conventions he registered as Ted Johnstone. Only on his professional writing did he use his real name.

In describing him, Short stated, "In a way, David's kind of demeanor, his style and his look, he was very much almost like a real life Illya Kuryakin. In thinking of Illya Kuryakin in the first few episodes of the first season of U.N.C.L.E. where he's a little bit more energetic and open, that kind of echoes David's look and personality because he had that same kind of interest in gadgets and technology and how things worked. But yet in real big social situations he was rather quiet, and kind of mysterious and aloof."

Besides the U.N.C.L.E. books and his science fiction novel, McDaniel also wrote one of the three novels based on THE PRISONER television series, as well as a science fiction novel AGENT OF T.E.R.R.A. In the '70s he also worked as a cameraman and freelance script writer, and was working on a script for QUINCY in 1977. On October 31, 1977, McDaniel died from a cerebral hemorrhage caused by an accidental fall in his home. He was 38 at the time of his death.

SCIENCE FICTION CONNECTION

David McDaniel wasn't the only Ace science fiction author whom Terry Carr turned to when he wanted to inject new blood into the U.N.C.L.E. novels. Carr recognized that for a series to be successful, it couldn't just trade on the characters but had to deliver the goods in the form of exciting and colorful adventures which the fans would enjoy enough to want to buy the next one.

Joan Hunter Holly (who wrote as J. Hunter Holly prior to 1970, in the finest tradition of obscuring her gender, just as Andre Norton did in the '50s when she wrote under the name Andrew Norton), wrote #10: THE ASSASSINATION AFFAIR. From 1966 to 1970 her writing career was put on hold while she battled a brain tumor but she recovered and began writing again in the '70s. A sec-

ACE BOOKS / G-617 / 50c

THE MAN FROM U.N.C.L.E.

NUMBER 9

The Diving Dames Affair

Solo and Illya infiltrate a secret THRUSH base in Brazil in an exciting new spy thriller by Peter Leslie.

ACE BOOKS / G-590 / 50c

THE MAN FROM U.N.C.L.E.

6

Illya and Napoleon battle their most fantastic enemy, in this chilling new adventure by David McDaniel.

The Vampire Affair

ond U.N.C.L.E. novel by her, THE WOLVES AND THE LAMB AFFAIR, was written in 1970 but rejected by Ace because they had already decided to cancel the series. It was published in a fanzine format, with her cooperation, in 1977. Holly died in 1982 at the age of 50.

Robert "Buck" Coulson, along with his wife Juanita, were editors of the 1965 Hugo Award winning fanzine YANDRO. In THE RAINBOW AFFAIR, author David McDaniel had two characters named "Buck DeWeese" and "Gene Coulson," after writers Gene DeWeese and Buck Coulson. Coulson and DeWeese wrote together under the pseudonym "Thomas Stratton" and authored the Ace U.N.C.L.E. books #11: THE INVISIBILITY AFFAIR and #12: THE MIND-TWISTERS AFFAIR. They weren't real U.N.C.L.E. fans and just wrote the books for the opportunity to get published, and paid. Their presentation of Solo and Kuryakin is basically as representatives of an exotic police agency.

THE INVISIBLE DIRIGIBLE AFFAIR

While McDaniel chose far-flung settings around the world, J. Hunter Holly and Coulson/DeWeese stuck close to home. Thus novels 10, 11 & 12 were set in the mid-west, in Michigan, Wisconsin and Indiana. On the other hand, since Solo and Kuryakin were based out of New York one would expect that their territory of assignment would be North America.

Since it had already been established in the television series that U.N.C.L.E. had branch offices around the world, one would logically assume that those offices would deal with problems in their own neck of the woods. But just as James Bond followed leads which took him to the United States in GOLDFINGER, so do Napoleon and Illya follow a trail which is international in scope.

Coulson and DeWeese wanted their first "Thomas Stratton" novel dedicated to "my wives and child," an inside joke virtually none of the readers would have understood. But Ace wouldn't go along with that and instead the dedication is the simple: To serendipity. They also wanted Ace #11: THE INVISIBILITY AFFAIR to be called THE INVISIBLE DIRIGIBLE AFFAIR, but that was nixed, too. Strangely enough, in spite of Ace dropping the word dirigible from the title they showcase the aircraft dramatically on the first page in bold letters which state: An Invisible Dirigible? If they wanted to keep the dirigible concept a secret the publishers had a strange way of going about it.

THE BRITISH CONNECTION

John T(for Thomas) Phillifent was a British author who wrote Ace U.N.C.L.E. #5: THE MAD SCIENTIST AFFAIR, also #19: THE POWER CUBE AFFAIR and #20: THE CORFU AFFAIR. Phillifent was a planning engineer for the English Electrical Board who also wrote science fiction, so his U.N.C.L.E. novels leaned on the technical side of storytelling for the menace and the adventure. His science fiction was also written under the pseudonym John Rackham, the name he was much more widely known under as an author. He wrote numerous science fiction novels including SPACE PUPPET (1954), JUPITER EQUILATERAL (1954), THE TOUCH OF EVIL (1963, a short story collection), DANGER FROM VEGA (1966), THE DOUBLE INVADERS (1967), DARK PLANET (1971) and others. He died in 1976 at the age of 60.

Peter Leslie was another English author whose career also included journalism and acting. Most of his books have science fiction overtones or are outright science fiction such as THE NIGHT OF THE TRILOBITES (1968), THE AUTUMN ACCELERATOR (1969) and THE PLASTIC MAGICIANS (1969).

Leslie's Ace U.N.C.L.E. books are #7: THE RADIOACTIVE CAMEL AFFAIR, #9: THE DIVING DAMES AFFAIR, #16: THE SPLINTERED SUNGLASSES AFFAIR, #18: THE UNFAIR FARE AFFAIR, and #23: THE FINGER IN THE SKY AFFAIR. Ace Books' U.N.C.L.E. #23 was the last one and due to the plummeting sales of the series by that time many stores didn't order the book so that it remains the most difficult U.N.C.L.E. novel to acquire. In 20 years I have never found a copy in a used book store but only found them through other collectors. It was 15 years after it was published before I even saw what one looked like. Leslie also wrote TV spin-off books based on THE AVENGERS and SECRET AGENT.

BACK TO AMERICA

Ron Ellik and Fredric Langley, friends of David McDaniel, were able through his assistance to pitch and sell an U.N.C.L.E. novel to editor Terry Carr which was published as #14: THE CROSS OF GOLD AFFAIR, in 1968. Ellik and Langley wrote the novel under the pseudonym "Fredric Davies." The book has a pleasant fannish feel which includes such contemporary references as Illya thinking that Mr. Waverly reminds him of Mr. Spock. "I bet when Mr. Waverly was younger he looked a lot like that, Illya thought. That is, if he had pointy ears, green skin and black bangs."

Ronald C. Ellik was a computer programmer and an sf fan who had known Terry Carr from his fandom days when Ellik and Carr co-edited the Hugo Award winning fanzine FANAC (from 1958 to '61). Ellik (in collaboration with Bill Evans) wrote the non-fiction book THE UNIVERSES OF E.E. SMITH which was published in 1966. Ron Ellik died in a car accident in 1968 the day before he was to be married.

While one source credits Fredric Langley as Ellik's partner on THE CROSS OF GOLD AFFAIR, THE SCIENCE FICTION ENCYCLOPEDIA edited by Peter Nicholls claims that one Steve Tolliver was Ellik's writing partner.

U.N.C.L.E. FANDOM

In spite of the cancellation of the series, U.N.C.L.E. fandom continued. David McDaniel, Bob Short, Don Simpson and Bill Mills remained died-in-the-wool U.N.C.L.E. fans who took advantage of the famous 1970 MGM auction to legally acquire original U.N.C.L.E. props, including the U.N.C.L.E. gun, THRUSH rifles and other choice items.

At the 1970 Westercon in Santa Barbara these U.N.C.L.E. enthusiasts not only showed off their collectibles but also screened a short "THRUSH training film" which had been written, directed and edited by David McDaniel. It featured Bob Short and Bill Mills in THRUSH uniforms attacking U.N.C.L.E. headquarters.

Inspired by the enthusiastic reception, they established their U.N.C.L.E. fan club, The Inner Circle II. They even published a fanzine called COMMUNIQUE which featured behind-the-scenes information about the series, its props, and anecdotes about various episodes. Their publication only lasted until 1972.

Although David McDaniel died in 1977 and never lived to see the 1983 television movie THE RETURN OF THE MAN

FROM U.N.C.L.E., Bob Short carried the flame and worked on the television movie as a consultant.

Today U.N.C.L.E. novels continue to be collected and read, and therefore David McDaniel's work is prized and preserved by his fans. With a major U.N.C.L.E. feature film now in the works, it will be interesting to see if any of the original U.N.C.L.E. novels will be reprinted when the film is released, possibly in 1995 or so.

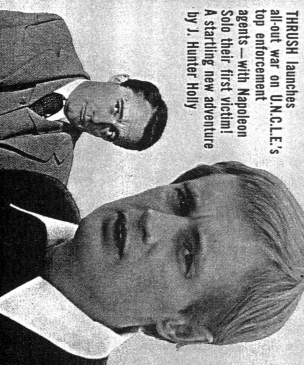

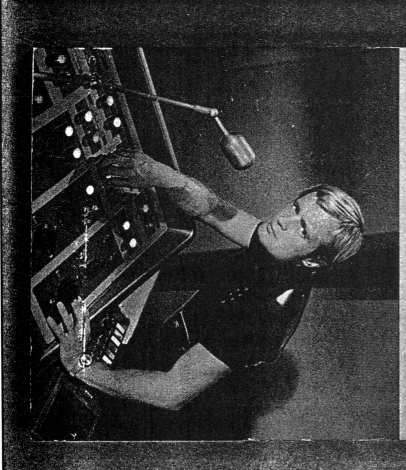

This chapter is a rare look behind-the-scenes which reveals how the U.N.C.L.E. TV tie-in magazines were written and the real names of the authors (some now well known) who wrote under the pseudonymous house name of Robert Hart Davis.

Chapter Fourteen

THE STORY BEHIND THE MAGAZINES

There were two U.N.C.L.E. magazines. THE MAN FROM U.N.C.L.E. ran for 24 monthly issues from February 1966 to January 1968.

THE GIRL FROM U.N.C.L.E. ran for 7 bi-monthly issues from December 1966 to December 1967. These were digest sized magazines, in size 5 1/2" X 7 1/2", with 144 pages. Each page had two columns of print. The magazines sold for 50 cents each.

They were published by the Leo Margulies Corporation and distributed by Publishers Distributing Corporation (PDC). The editor was Cylvia Kleinman (actually Cylvia K. Margulies, the wife of Leo, the publisher). H.N. Alden was listed as the Associate Editor. He was really Alden H. Norton who was working at Popular Publications at the time.

Publisher Leo Margulies was a fascinating character. He was born in Brooklyn in 1900. While at Columbia University he got a job as an office boy at Munsey Publications. He worked for Robert H. Davis, who had been a famous columnist for the NEW YORK SUN before becoming the preeminent editor for Munsey Magazines. He is credited with discovering O'Henry, Max Brand and Joseph Conrad. Davis talked Margulies into working full time as an editor at Munsey.

Ned Pines started Standard Magazines in 1931. He hired Leo Margulies as Editorial Director. In the titles of their magazines was the word THRILLING. So they were known as "The Thrilling Group." Leo was called "the little giant of the pulps" since he was short in stature but was held in high esteem. In 1942 he helped to establish the Popular Library part (to publish paperbacks) of the Pines organization. About 1950 he moved over to it. In 1956 he set up his own company to publish digest sized magazines. In addition to the U.N.C.L.E. magazines, he published MIKE SHAYNE,

By Albert Tonik

THE MAN FROM U.N.C.L.E.

MAGAZINE   JUNE   50c   PDC

NAPOLEON SOLO ★ ILLYA KURYAKIN

Invisibility is their deadly weapon as Wily MORLOCK THE GREAT and fiendish THRUSH conspire to take over a world of free men.

in —

THE VANISHING ACT AFFAIR
The New Complete U.N.C.L.E. Novel by
ROBERT HART DAVIS

Also:
ED LACY
DENNIS LYNDS
HARRY WHITTINGTON

ZANE GREY, CHARLIE CHAN, SHELL SCOTT, and others. Leo died in 1975 and Cylvia died in 1984.

BEHIND-THE-U.N.C.L.E.-SCENES

Each issue of the U.N.C.L.E. magazines contained a novella of between 60 and 90 pages featuring the U.N.C.L.E. characters. Most of the time black and white stills from the TV show were on the covers, both front and back. A different colored background was on the front cover of each issue, but the spines of all the issues were white. Hector Castellon did most of the line drawings in the interior of the magazines.

The author of the U.N.C.L.E. story in each issue was stated as Robert Hart Davis, which was actually just a house name as the stories were ghost-written by a variety of authors. I'll attempt to identify them when I discuss the story they wrote along with other background material. This information was gathered from the files at MGM, from the papers of Leo Margulies at the University of Oregon and from the files of various authors.

Every story had to be approved by MGM before it was published. The stories had to be original, not adaptations from the TV scripts because at that time MGM did not know how to handle royalty payments to the script writers. Also, nothing in the story could be interpreted as being derived from a James Bond book, in order to avoid trouble with Ian Fleming's estate. Moya Morin was the reader at MGM who either rejected the stories, approved them or suggested changes to them.

THE CONTRACT FROM U.N.C.L.E.

Leo Margulies and MGM agreed to a contract on September 8, 1965. The second season of the TV show started on September 17, 1965. The contract was signed on October 2, 1965. According to the terms, Margulies paid one cent to MGM for each copy (of each issue) sold up to 150,000 copies, and $.015 for any copies over that amount. He supplied 50 copies of each issue to MGM. A contract was signed with PDC on November 4. The publisher shipped to wholesalers around the country the number of copies specified by the distributor. The publisher paid for shipping. Seventy days after off-sale, which occurred 30 days after on-sale, the distributor paid to the publisher $.28 for each copy sold to a customer, except where the wholesaler paid less than $.32, in which case the distributor paid a corresponding lesser amount.

Leo Margulies called Dennis Lynds to author U.N.C.L.E. stories. For the past 3 years, Lynds had written MIKE SHAYNE novelettes for Leo. Dennis agreed to do six per year (half of them). For 30,000 words Leo agreed to pay $450 and up to the amount of $600 if the magazine made a profit.

On September 9, 1965, Margulies wrote to Lynds. By this time two of the Ace books had been published, those by Avallone and Whittington. Leo had a copy of the year-old NBC brochure which was used to sell the show to advertisers. These items, and watching the show, constituted the background used by the authors. Leo asked Lynds to select the titles of the first two stories since it was cheaper to print two covers at once. To Dennis Lynds he sent a list of 50 suggested titles. Leo liked THE HOWLING TEENAGERS AFFAIR. He had some suggestions for the story.

"Have a musical group, modeled on the Beatles, working for THRUSH, inflame toward

A LIST OF SUGGESTED AFFAIRS

THE ANGEL OF DEATH AFFAIR
THE FALLEN ANGEL AFFAIR
THE DEATH'S ANGEL AFFAIR
THE DEADLY SIN AFFAIR
THE CHINATOWN-HANOI AFFAIR
THE RIVIERA AFFAIR
THE COTE D'AZUR AFFAIR
THE UNSPEAKABLE AFFAIR
THE UNMENTIONABLE AFFAIR
THE TARNISHED LADY AFFAIR
THE BRIDGE OF SIGHS AFFAIR
THE HEARTBREAK HOUSE AFFAIR
THE SAVAGE BEAST AFFAIR
THE WHISPERER AFFAIR
THE WHISPERING MAN AFFAIR
THE DEADLY WHISPER AFFAIR
THE BREATH OF DEATH AFFAIR
THE NEEDLE OF DEATH AFFAIR
THE GRAVEYARD WATCH AFFAIR
THE LONESOME DEAD AFFAIR
THE KILL AND TELL AFFAIR
THE POLISH CORRIDOR AFFAIR
THE LONELY DUNES AFFAIR
THE FRENCH QUARTER AFFAIR
THE ROMAN ROAD AFFAIR
THE LADY FROM HELL AFFAIR
THE ANGEL FROM HELL AFFAIR
THE DREADFUL BEDFUL AFFAIR
THE LONE WOLF AFFAIR
THE ROAD TO NOWHERE AFFAIR
THE ASIAN CORRIDOR AFFAIR
THE AFRICAN MASQUE AFFAIR
THE WHITENED SEPULCHRE AFFAIR
THE WINDSWEPT WOODS AFFAIR
THE KISS OF DEATH AFFAIR
THE CURIOUS CALL GIRL AFFAIR
THE LONELY LAKE AFFAIR
THE VELVET CORD AFFAIR
THE WORLD'S END AFFAIR
THE SPANISH STEPS AFFAIR
THE BLUE TRAIN AFFAIR
THE CALAIS CROSSING AFFAIR
THE LOST CANYON AFFAIR
THE SMALL BACK ROOM AFFAIR
THE FATAL FLAME AFFAIR
THE OLD WIVE'S MALE AFFAIR
THE YEGG IN HIS BIER AFFAIR
THE AWFUL DEATH AFFAIR
THE LADY FROM HADES AFFAIR
THE PURGATORY AFFAIR
THE HOWLING TEENAGERS AFFAIR

violence teenagers all over the world via some chemical. The results: in the Palladium a mod dove from the balcony, in Shea Stadium a girl screamed and died, in Rome a paparazzi held a knife to an old man's throat. Include all sorts of gadgets and experimental drugs; especially the communicator, a plastic and metal rectangle that fits into the palm of the hand."

On September 14, 1965, Lynds replied to Margulies. His analysis was, "THRUSH has only one aim, to acquire POWER to take over the world. They do this in one of 4 ways; direct thrusts for power, develop or steal a weapon, build their funds, destroy or take over U.N.C.L.E. The stories should be like the TV scripts; very episodic, with rapid changes of scene to provide many points of view." He agreed to do THE HOWLING TEENAGERS AFFAIR as the first story, but "each incident had to have some hidden meaning for POWER; important men dying with THRUSH people taking their place, the acquisition of vital documents, etc."

THE FIRST MAGAZINE

For a second story, Lynds suggested THE MOONS OF VENUS AFFAIR. "An U.N.C.L.E. agent is skulking around, a sphere floats by, poof, he dies, uttering the words, 'The moons of Venus.' But Venus has no moons. Solo and Kuryakin discover that THRUSH has a new gas, which makes plants give off carbon dioxide instead of oxygen, thus smothering nearby people." [This, of course, ignored the fact that at night plants already give off carbon dioxide as they only give off oxygen during the day under the stimulus of sunlight and the resulting photosynthesis.]

As alternatives he suggested THE WORLD'S END AFFAIR (the name of a London pub) or THE UNSPEAKABLE AFFAIR (a THRUSH chemical renders U.N.C.L.E. agents mute).

Dennis Lynds finished THE HOWLING TEENAGERS AFFAIR by September 24, 1965. He stated, "I feel that Solo and Kuryakin have to be very bright boys, always beating the enemy and yet getting out-witted in turn." He invented THRUSH agent Maxine Trent, and used her in most of his stories. On October 8 the manuscript was approved by MGM except for one suggested change. "Illya should not enter the underground complex of Marcus Fitzhugh via a ventilation duct, but by means of a cleverly disguised inspection ladder running down the elevator shaft." There were some mistakes in the story which were not caught for months. Instead of using the section number and names from the NBC brochure, he used the incorrect ones from the introduction of the first Ace book. He did not use the name Heather McNab but the name of the actress, May Heatherly.

The cover was proofed about October 15. On November 12, 1965, Dennis Lynds was paid $450. The cover was printed on November 24th. The magazine hit the newsstands at the beginning of January 1966 with 250,000 copies. By April 25 they had the results. The magazine sold well in California and the East, but the overall statistics were not good. They did not lose money but they had to reduce the print run. Dennis Lynds never received the $600 per story, which caused a little bitterness. After doing five stories he quit, but came back the next year.

A VARIETY OF GHOSTS

In the meantime, publisher Leo Margulies knew he needed a second author (Lynds was origi-nally intending to write only half of the annual output, even before he decided to quit). He went to literary agent Scott Meredith and obtained the services of Harry Whittington and John Jakes. Whittington, who had done the second Ace book, started THE BEAUTY AND BEAST AFFAIR on October, 1965. On October 20th it was rejected by MGM because the premise resembled that used in ON HER MAJESTY'S SECRET SERVICE. MGM said that in the future, an outline should be submitted for approval before the novella was written. Leo liked the story about poisoning livestock with anthrax. He kept it, modified the names, and printed it as THE SHIP OF HORROR in the February 1968 issue of MIKE SHAYNE MYSTERY MAGAZINE.

What about the second issue of the U.N.C.L.E. magazine? Harry Whittington sat down and wrote another version of THE BEAUTY AND BEAST AFFAIR. He finished it November 13, 1965. It was not okayed until November 22nd because MGM's lawyer was on vacation. In the meantime, frantic because of deadlines, Cylvia had ordered it set in type. So the March 1966 issue went out on time. Harry was paid $450 on November 26. In the story he used Wanda Mae Kim as a new agent even though

THE MAN FROM U.N.C.L.E.

MAGAZINE

SEPT. 50c PDC

NAPOLEON SOLO ★ ILLYA KURYAKIN

No man knew them! All men feared them!
Only our master spy hunters stood between
THRUSH and their control of a free world.

THE BRAINWASH AFFAIR

A New Complete U.N.C.L.E. Novel by ROBERT HART DAVIS

MURDER IN SAIGON

A War Time Spy Novelet by TOM H. MORIARTY

she was classified as a receptionist in the NBC brochure. In the Ace book, Harry had invented the code names Sonny and Bubba for Napoleon and Illya to use while talking to one another over the communicators. So who used these names? Dennis Lynds did.

The third issue, April 1966, contained THE UNSPEAKABLE AFFAIR. Leo asked Dennis Lynds for this one on September 17, 1965. Lynds began it sometime in October and finished it on November 1st. He put aside and never returned to THE MOONS OF VENUS AFFAIR. On November 9th, Cylvia wrote to Dennis and asked him to vary his endings. "So far the endings have been far away from a city, in a great barren, isolated area." The manuscript was approved on November 30th (remember the lawyer's vacation). It could have made the second issue of the magazine if MGM had rejected the second version of THE BEAUTY AND BEAST AFFAIR. Dennis was paid $450 on December 20.

JOHN JAKES— U.N.C.L.E. FAN

The fourth issue, May 1966, had THE WORLD'S END AFFAIR. Those that have paid attention up to this point would say the author was Dennis Lynds. Wrong! The author was John Jakes! John states that he was contacted by Scott Meredith and took on the work because, "I was a prime fan of the series." The story was completed before November 18, 1965. MGM approved it on November 30th. On February 14, 1966, John was paid $450. He invented Jacques, the projectionist, whom he used in all his stories. John Jakes, of course, went on to become a best-selling author of historical novels in the seventies and eighties.

In April when the magazine came out, MGM was miffed. The still on the back cover was a picture of Dorothy Provine between David McCallum and Robert Vaughn. Provine was not under contract as the others were and so could not be used to publicize the show. Back in February, MGM had negotiated with her for the role of April Dancer, but the deal collapsed. Someone had been premature when they sent that photograph to the Margulies.

In the fifth issue, June 1966, was THE VANISHING ACT AFFAIR by Dennis Lynds. On November 16, 1965 he began to think about this story which he called THE END OF THE WORLD AFFAIR. On

December 3rd he finished a three page outline. MGM approved it on December 22nd. On that date, Cylvia changed the name to THE VANISHING ACT AFFAIR since the previous name was too close to the one used by John Jakes. The story was finished on January 10, 1966. The manuscript was sent to MGM on January 16th and approved provisionally on January 25th. They wanted one scene modified. "Instead of Solo freeing himself with a blowtorch which he maneuvers with his teeth, let him find some sharp abrasive or abrasive surface against which he can fray the ropes." Dennis was paid $450 on February 21st.

U.N.C.L.E./SHADOW CONNECTION?

In the sixth issue, July 1966, was THE GHOST RIDERS AFFAIR by Harry Whittington, who began this story on November 20, 1965. He finished the outline on November 22nd. MGM approved the 3 page outline after December 21st. The news did not reach Harry until January 17, 1966, but in the meantime he continued and finished the story on January 20th. MGM approved it on February 1st. Harry was paid $450 on April 7th.

THE ATOMIC DIAMONDS AFFAIR by Harry Whittington was begun on January 16, 1966. He turned in either the story or more probably the outline on February 1st to Scott Meredith. Nothing else was ever heard of this story.

The seventh issue, August 1966, contained THE CAT AND MOUSE AFFAIR by Dennis Lynds. Dennis began this on February 21st. He turned the outline in on February 23rd. MGM approved the 3 page outline on February 28th. After a bout with the flu, the manuscript was finished on March 23rd. MGM did not approve it until April 19th because Moya Morin was on vacation. Dennis was paid $450 on May 14th.

At this time Belmont was issuing a series of paperbacks about the adventures of The Shadow written by Maxwell Grant (another house name). Dennis Lynds wrote these stories. No one knew this until some astute fans began noticing similarities. THE CAT AND MOUSE AFFAIR takes place on the island of Zambala off the northeast coast of South America. The action in THE SHADOW'S REVENGE, from October 1965, occurs near the city, Zambala, in a new country in Africa.

CAUGHT IN THE ACT!

However, many coincidences occur in MARK OF THE SHADOW published in May 1966. The story opens with a shooting in a disreputable motel in Santa Carla. The police arrive and find that the Mayor had killed a Mafia leader. It was a case of self-defense. The Mayor refuses exoneration. He insists on suspending himself while the law follows a regular investigation. Then the District Attorney is killed. The suspected murderer is a Mafia member. He is put in jail where he commits suicide. A Crime Commission is gathered, a member being New York Police Commissioner Weston. His friend, Lamont Cranston, accompanies him. Thus The Shadow enters the case. The Shadow discovers an organization, CYPHER, has been hired to do the killings. The culprit is the head of the Crime Commission.

THE CAT AND MOUSE AFFAIR opens with a shooting in a hotel. The police discover the Premier of Zambala has killed a leader of the opposition in self-defense. He refuses exoneration, suspends himself and demands an investigation. An international tribunal is assembled. The Security Chief is killed by a member of the opposition. The killer dies escaping prison. In the end Solo and Kuryakin discover that it was all a plot of the chairman of the tribunal.

The publisher, Leo Margulies, was upset. On August 13, 1966, Dennis assured him "even though the first few scenes are similar, all the rest of the action is completely different."

In the September 1966 issue, the eighth, was THE BRAINWASH AFFAIR by Harry Whittington. Harry began this story on September 9, 1965. Leo must have contacted him right after contacting Lynds. For some reason, Harry put it aside and did THE BEAUTY AND BEAST AFFAIR. He sent THE BRAINWASH AFFAIR to Scott Meredith on March 25, 1966. The manuscript was sent to MGM on April 8th. It was not approved until April 28 because of Morin's vacation. There is no indication that an outline was done. Harry was paid $450 on June 27th.

The ninth issue, October 1966, contained THE MOBY DICK AFFAIR by John Jakes. The outline was sent to MGM in April, but the approval was delayed because of Morin's vacation. The manuscript was approved by MGM on May 6.

John was paid $450 on August 29.

A FAVOR FOR THE PUBLISHER

In the tenth issue, November 1966, was THE THRUSH FROM THRUSH AFFAIR by Dennis Lynds. On February 21st, Leo suggested to Dennis that he try a story called THE GIRL FROM THRUSH AFFAIR, but Dennis had started on THE CAT AND MOUSE AFFAIR. On March 28, Cylvia suggested THE THRUSH FROM THRUSH AFFAIR. She had a friend, Greta Keller, "who is a dazzling chanteuse (in the manner of Marlene Dietrich and Edith Piaf). This winter she was in Hollywood. The writer of the inferior THE ROUND TABLE AFFAIR that was on TV last Friday, Robert Hill, took her to the U.N.C.L.E. set to watch some filming. The producer said that if they ever had a part in a story for Greta, they'd cast her. She'd like nothing better as she loves the show. Can you include a part for her in your story? Have her sing a code to a THRUSH pal in the audience."

Dennis agreed to "give Miss Keller a hell of a bloody role" on April 7th. He sent the outline on April 25th. MGM approved the 3 page outline on April 26. MGM approved the manuscript on May 17th. Dennis was paid $450 on July 22, 1966.

The eleventh issue, December 1966, contained THE GOLIATH AFFAIR by John Jakes. The manuscript was approved by MGM on July 22nd. John was paid $450 on October 19th.

On August 3, 1966, Cylvia sent MGM an outline of THE SANTA CLAUSE AFFAIR. MGM rejected it on August 9th. "The idea of toy weapons being as lethal as full-scale ones was used in a recently completed MAN FROM U.N.C.L.E. segment in which THRUSH at the flick of a switch converts seemingly innocent toys into death-dealing weapons."

In the twelfth issue, January 1967, was the story THE LIGHT-KILL AFFAIR by Harry Whittington. Harry began it on July 29, 1966. He mailed a 5 page outline to Scott Meredith on August 3rd. MGM approved it with additional suggestions by Cylvia about August 25. Harry completed the story on September 29th. MGM approved the manuscript on October 4th. Harry was paid $450 on November 10th.

GHOST WRITERS

In the thirteenth issue, February 1967, was THE

DEADLY DARK AFFAIR by John Jakes. John submitted a 3 page outline for a story entitled THE BLACKOUT AFFAIR. MGM approved it along with some suggestions from Cylvia about August 25th. The manuscript was approved by MGM on October 24th. At a later time the title was changed to THE DEADLY DARK AFFAIR. John was paid $450 on December 2, 1966.

The fourteenth issue, March 1967, contained THE HUNGRY WORLD AFFAIR by Talmage Powell. In October 1966 MGM approved a 4 page outline entitled THE STARVATION AFFAIR. A manuscript, with the same name, from Scott Meredith, was approved on November 18th. Talmage was paid $450 on January 11, 1967.

In the fifteenth issue, April 1967, was THE DOLLS OF DEATH AFFAIR by John Jakes. John submitted a 2 page outline entitled THE U.F.O. AFFAIR in late October 1966. MGM approved it but suggested it to be called THE FLYING SAUCER AFFAIR. "We have just filmed a GIRL FROM U.N.C.L.E. show called THE U.F.O. AFFAIR." In December, John sent the story entitled THE DOLLS OF DEATH AFFAIR. MGM approved it on December 22nd. John was paid $450 on March 3, 1967.

In the sixteenth issue, May 1967, was THE SYNTHETIC STORM AFFAIR by I.G. Edmonds. MGM approved a 4 page outline early in December 1966. On December 2nd, Meredith asked Ivy "to convert this story from a GIRL (from U.N.C.L.E., written for the companion title) to a MAN (from U.N.C.L.E.) story. Leo told me that the author working on the present MAN story had a serious accident and will not be able to deliver on time." Ivy wrote this story from December 25th to January 6, 1967. MGM approved the manuscript on January 12th. Ivy was paid $450 on March 27th.

DENNIS LYNDS RETURNS

In the seventeenth issue, June 1967, was the story THE UGLY MAN AFFAIR by John Jakes. Jakes submitted a 2 page outline entitled THE DRACULA AFFAIR. MGM approved it in January, but thought it should have a different name like THE BLOOD SHOULD BE THICKER THAN WATER AFFAIR. MGM approved the manuscript entitled THE UGLY MAN AFFAIR on March 1st. John was paid $500 on May 11th. He does not remember why his payment was increased.

July 1967, the eighteenth issue, was THE ELECTRONIC FRANKENSTEIN AFFAIR by Frank Belknap Long. Long submitted an 8 page outline named THE NEW FRANKENSTEIN AFFAIR. MGM okayed it in December, 1966. On February 14th MGM wrote to Cylvia, "Thanks for reminding the printer about the change of direction." The only change I can find is that the logo no longer spreads across the front cover but is confined to a box, two-thirds of the width of the cover.

The finished manuscript, named THE ELECTRONIC FRANKENSTEIN AFFAIR, was not approved by MGM until February 28, 1967. I think the delay of this story was the cause of I.G. Edmonds changing THE SYNTHETIC STORM AFFAIR from a GIRL to a MAN FROM U.N.C.L.E. story. Cylvia did not remember any accident happening to Frank, but remembered this story being on time. Frank was paid $450 on March 3rd.

The nineteenth issue, August 1967, contained THE GENGHIS KHAN AFFAIR by Dennis Lynds. Dennis was still writing MIKE SHAYNE novelettes for Leo and needed money. Cylvia suggested doing an U.N.C.L.E. story on January 10th. On January 24th, MGM approved a 4 page outline for THE CHINESE THRUSH AFFAIR. On January 27 Dennis said, "Due to news from China, I will change it to hint that THRUSH started all this Civil War trouble." On February 8th, MGM partially approved the manuscript. "When Illya sabotages the control mechanism (avoid mentioning the steering system) of the rocket THRUSH is launching, let the missile blow up on the pad as in the outline rather than being launched to fall back to earth ten miles away." MGM approved the changes February 13, 1967. Dennis was paid $450 on March 3rd.

THE OFFICIAL UNOFFICIAL TRUTH

Cylvia thought that the title was similar to THE THRUSH FROM THRUSH AFFAIR, so she changed it. MGM approved the title THE GENGHIS KHAN AFFAIR on March 6th. At the same time Cylvia asked for "the definition of the initials, THRUSH." MGM replied, "There never was an official definition but (David) McDaniel in an Ace Book invented the colorful The Technological Hierarchy for the

THE MAN FROM U.N.C.L.E.

MAGAZINE MAY 50c PDC

NAPOLEON SOLO
ILLYA KURYAKIN

AMERICA'S
FAVORITE
U.N.C.L.E.s
HAVE A DATE
WITH DANGER!

in —

THE
SYNTHETIC
STORM
AFFAIR

A NEW Complete Novel by
ROBERT HART DAVIS

Removal of Undesirables and the Subjugation of Humanity."

In February 1967 Charles Ventura submitted a 4 page outline for a MAN FROM U.N.C.L.E. story called THE GYPSY CHAIN AFFAIR. MGM approved it but no more was heard of it.

The twentieth issue, September 1967, contained THE MAN FROM YESTERDAY AFFAIR by John Jakes. In April MGM okayed a 2 page outline. On May 16th MGM approved the manuscript. John was paid $500 on July 10th.

The twenty-first issue, October 1967, had THE MIND-SWEEPER AFFAIR by Dennis Lynds. Dennis gave a synopsis of this story early in February in a few sentences. On February 17th, Cylvia said, "We have two MAN stories on hand and will not need another until the middle of March but get the outline approved early." On March 10th MGM okayed a 5 page outline for THE BRAIN PICKER AFFAIR. On March 13th, Cylvia asked for some changes. "The June MIKE SHAYNE story has a similar title, change yours. The mind reading device is excellent, but get it into the story earlier. I will not need the story until the end of April." On April 11th Dennis sent THE MIND-SWEEPER AFFAIR to MGM.

MGM approved the manuscript on April 17th. Dennis was paid $450 on June 14th. On that date, the August copy was printed and bound.

A TWO YEAR ADVENTURE ENDS

In the twenty-second issue, November 1967, THE VOL-CANO BOX AFFAIR by Richard Curtis appeared. In February, Ace Books had submitted an outline by Richard called THE EARTHQUAKE AFFAIR. It was rejected because of the TV episodes "The Cherry Blossom Affair" (volcano erupter) and "The Yo-Ho-Ho and a Bottle of Rum Affair" (tidal wave machine). MGM said, "There could be no story using a THRUSH machine to cause volcanic eruptions, earthquakes, or tidal waves."

Later in February MGM approved a 2 page outline for Cylvia from Richard for THE VOLCANO BOX AFFAIR (an enhanced laser beam to drill through the earth's mantle to start a volcano). On June 2nd MGM approved the manu-script. Richard was paid $450 on July 26th.

In the twenty-third issue, December 1967, was THE PIL-LARS OF SALT AFFAIR by Bill

Pronzini. Bill's agent was Scott Meredith. MGM approved a 6 page outline in February. MGM okayed the manuscript on June 6th. Bill was paid $450 on October 4th. He used the actress May Heatherly instead of her character Heather McNab, as did Lynds in an earlier story. Solo and Kuryakin wind up in the hospital because Bill hates stories with violent situations and the main characters are never harmed.

January 1968, the twenty-fourth issue, was the final published issue of the MAN FROM U.N.C.L.E. magazine. It features THE MILLION MONSTERS AFFAIR by I.G. Edmonds. Ivy submitted a 10 page outline to MGM on April 24, 1967. MGM okayed it in May. However, they warned, "It is very similar to THE HOWLING TEENAGERS AFFAIR by Dennis Lynds." On July 19th, MGM approved the manuscript. This story was written before THE SINISTER SATELLITE AFFAIR but appeared after it. In Cylvia's records, Ivy was paid $450 on October 8th. However on May 29, 1969, Scott Meredith states, "I have been trying to collect this fee for more than a year and finally the Margulies have agreed to pay from funds for Portuguese rights."

THE GIRL FROM U.N.C.L.E.

December 1966, the first issue of THE GIRL FROM U.N.C.L.E., had THE SHEIK OF ARABY AFFAIR by Richard Deming. In June, 1966, Leo had been offered a contract by MGM to publish this magazine. He did not want it but thought he must accept it to protect his investment in THE MAN FROM U.N.C.L.E. magazine. The contract was signed in early August. The terms of the contract were the same as the MAN FROM U.N.C.L.E. magazine.

On July 21st, Deming sent a 9 page outline to MGM. He suggested "it be shown to the story editor of the TV show because I could turn it into a script easily." MGM okayed it on July 26th. Deming sent a manuscript to MGM on August 13th. He said, "There might be some mistakes since Leo was in a rush and I did it in 6 days instead of my usual 10 days." MGM approved it on August 15th.

All of this took place before THE GIRL FROM U.N.C.L.E. television show began, so these spy stories are straight adventures. Richard was paid $525 for 35,000 words on August 31st. The magazine hit the newsstands on Thursday, October 6th. In the table of contents the story is listed as SHEIK FROM ARABY AFFAIR. At the end of the story, Solo and Kuryakin appear.

The second issue of THE GIRL FROM U.N.C.L.E., February 1967, contained THE VELVET VOICE AFFAIR by Richard Deming. The December 1966 issue had announced next THE DEADLY DRUG AFFAIR, which did not appear until the fourth issue. Richard sent a 4 page outline for an untitled novel #2 to MGM on September 21st. MGM approved it on September 27th. Deming sent the manuscript to MGM on November 1st. MGM approved THE VELVET VOICE AFFAIR on November 7th. Richard was paid $525 on December 2nd.

The third issue, April 1967, contained THE BURNING AIR AFFAIR by I.G. Edmonds. Cylvia sent a 20 page outline to MGM on October 27, 1966. MGM okayed it on November 2nd. Cylvia sent the manuscript to MGM on November 22nd. MGM approved it on November 28th. "It varied from the outline." Ivy Edmonds was paid $525 on January 11, 1967.

DISAGREEMENTS

Cylvia sent to MGM on December 6, 1966, an outline for a GIRL FROM U.N.C.L.E. story, Charles Ventura's THE DEADLY DOWAGERS AFFAIR. MGM rejected it on December 9th. "We have a TV script for a GIRL FROM U.N.C.L.E. story about a group of people who discover a rejuvenation system and they blackmail wives of important world figures." "The Fountain of Youth Affair" was scheduled to begin filming December 15th.

The fourth issue, June 1967, has THE DEADLY DRUG AFFAIR by Richard Deming. Richard submitted a 13 page outline on August 20, 1966. MGM rejected it on September 1st and stated, "In GOLDFINGER, there was an attempt to pollute the water supply of Fort Knox with a nerve drug to put the population to sleep for three days or to death. You can not take over a country by means of a drug which affects people's minds so they lose their ability to reason. Do not start the story with U.N.C.L.E. and THRUSH agents meeting at a drug manufacturers' convention." Are they referring to the biochemists' meeting at the start of THE MAD SCIENTIST AFFAIR, Ace Books #5 as the other point of conflict?

On September 21st, Richard submitted another outline to MGM (THE VELVET VOICE AFFAIR). He wrote, "I have not read GOLDFINGER nor seen the movie. Can I use an invisible, odorless gas instead of drugging the water supply? Can April and Mark meet the THRUSH agents at a scientific conclave instead of a drug convention?" MGM replied on September 27th, "You can't use such a gas. In the motion picture, Pussy Galor's Flying Circus releases an invisible nerve gas over Fort Knox. It is okay to put the drug into bread or the milk supply. You can have U.N.C.L.E. and THRUSH agents meet at a scientific conclave of say, psychiatrists, if it is not the opening scene and is not held in a city, but at a country resort." On December 3rd, Richard sent a manuscript to MGM. MGM approved it on December 6th. Richard was paid $525 on May 8, 1967.

A BRIEF RUN NEARS ITS END

In the fifth issue, August 1967, was THE MESMERIZING MIST AFFAIR by Charles Ventura. After striking out with THE DEADLY DOWAGER AFFAIR, Charles tried again. A 4 page outline was approved by MGM in December 1966. The story went to MGM on January 30, 1967. MGM partially approved the manuscript on February 3rd. They objected "to the effect of the drug in the anesthetizing mist being like hypnosis. It should be more like a drugged trance, with the victims obedient and submissive." Cylvia paid Charles $525 on February 9th.

In the sixth issue, October 1967, was THE STOLEN SPACEMAN AFFAIR by I.G. Edmonds. A 13 page outline was sent to MGM on January 30th. On February 3rd MGM conditionally okayed it. "When April and Mark are fleeing from THRUSH by motorboat do not pour gasoline on the river, lay a smoke screen instead." This was no doubt because of a similar scene on FROM RUSSIA WITH LOVE. Scott Meredith sent the manuscript to MGM on March 20th. MGM approved it on March 24th even though it varied in some details from the outline. Ivy was paid $525 on August 1, 1967.

The seventh issue, December 1967, had THE SINISTER SATELLITE AFFAIR by I.G. Edmonds. Ivy says, "I was asked to star all four U.N.C.L.E. agents in this story." A 5 page outline was submitted to MGM in July for either magazine. It was approved by MGM on July 12th. The manuscript was submitted to MGM on August

17th. MGM approved it on August 22nd. Ivy was paid $450 on November 28th.

THE UNPUBLISHED AFFAIRS

THE VANISHING CITY AFFAIR by I.G. Edmonds was a GIRL story. On April 24, 1967 a 10 page outline was sent to MGM. MGM approved it on May 12th but made the following observations. "By utilizing magnetic fields THRUSH bends light rays around San Francisco causing it to disappear. April and Mark enter the city via a submarine. With no light getting to the city it's like night. THRUSH plans to loot the city to afford a bigger generator to blanket the earth to blackmail the world. April makes the truck carrying the generator go over a cliff. In THE INVISIBILITY AFFAIR, Ace #11, THRUSH steals the OTSMID which turns objects invisible by making them transparent. THRUSH starts a revolution in South America by landing troops in an invisible dirigible."

Ivy changed this into a MAN FROM U.N.C.L.E. manuscript and sent it to MGM on August 7th. MGM approved it on August 10th. It was scheduled for the February 1968 issue, which was never printed. By November 1967 Margulies knew the TV show was to be canceled and he would stop the magazines because of poor sales. They never paid for this story. Ivy said, "The story opened with the men of U.N.C.L.E. flying into San Francisco from a foreign port when the city vanished." This was another story written before THE SINISTER SATELLITE AFFAIR.

THE SCORCHING SEA AFFAIR by I.G. Edmonds was a MAN FROM U.N.C.L.E. story. MGM approved a 20 page outline on July 25, 1967. This story dealt with breaking through the thin earth crust at the pole, letting magma out, melting the polar cap and causing flooding of coastal areas with resultant weather changes.

THE UNFINISHED AFFAIRS

THE HOMING-HORNETS OF DEATH AFFAIR by Harry Whittington was a MAN FROM U.N.C.L.E. story. Harry submitted an outline on August 28, 1967 but it never got to MGM.

THE TRAITOR FROM THRUSH AFFAIR by I.G. Edmonds was a MAN FROM U.N.C.L.E. story. On September

5, 1967 an outline was sent to MGM. MGM approved the 11 page outline on September 15th.

THE SHANGRI LA AFFAIR by Dennis Lynds was a MAN FROM U.N.C.L.E. story. A 5 page outline was sent to MGM on October 10, 1967. MGM approved it on October 13. Lynds proposed writing about a vanishing island and piracy back on April 11, 1967. In September he proposed THE ROBOT AFFAIR about THRUSH kidnapping experts, blanking their memory but preserving their knowledge, giving them new IDs and selling them to needy countries (rejected by Cylvia). Then came the story about people hypnotized to believe they have regained their youth.

THE RIP VAN WINKLE AFFAIR by I.G. Edmonds was a MAN FROM U.N.C.L.E. story. An outline was sent to MGM on October 16, 1967. MGM approved the 13 page outline plus the first 14 pages of the story (the first 2 chapters) on October 24th.

The last issue of the GIRL FROM U.N.C.L.E. magazine announced that THE UTTERLY INCOMPREHENSIBLE AFFAIR would appear in the next issue. Since no such story with that title was ever submitted to MGM, was this an inside joke?

Thus ended the magazines, canceled along with the television series which spawned them. It would be interesting to draw a time diagram to observe what happens at the same time in different stories. The timeline for a single story overlaps that of others. Also a synopsis for each story would be interesting, but really, this chapter is already long enough!

Beginning in the late 1970's, two men who had some professional experience in Hollywood embarked on a hard fought campaign to bring THE MAN FROM U.N.C.L.E. to the big screen. The following is the story of their attempt and all of the difficulties they encountered along the way.

Chapter Fifteen

THE UNCLE THAT ALMOST WAS

"Of all the words of mice and men,
The saddest are these,
'It might have been'! "

Those feelings of resignation and fading hope were experienced at some level by Danny Biederman and Robert Short in early 1983 when they watched THE RETURN OF THE MAN FROM U.N.C.L.E. in the form of a two-hour TV movie on CBS. The reason they regarded the long-awaited return Solo and Illya as a mixed blessing is that they'd been trying to launch a return of U.N.C.L.E. on their own since 1979. But instead of a scaled-down TV movie it would have been a full blown feature film done by people who had a great affection for the old series and wanted to do justice to it on a grand scale.

Besides being longtime U.N.C.L.E. fans, Danny Biederman and Robert Short have independent credits of their own in the film community.

Danny Biederman has written and produced over fifty featurettes, documentaries and commercials, some of which have won awards. This includes "A Spy For All Seasons," which is a behind-the-scenes short on the making of the James Bond film DIAMONDS ARE FOREVER. He also sold a comedy script titled CHERRIES OF FIRE as a motion picture project and worked with French director Claude LeLouch, studying under him during the production of his first American film, ANOTHER MAN, ANOTHER CHANCE. He was a writer and an editor for Irving Wallace and has had work published in THE PEOPLE'S ALMANAC and THE BOOK OF LISTS.

In collaboration with Bob Short, Biederman penned an unproduced script for the series GAVILAN, but the show was canceled before the episode could be filmed. That series starred Robert Urich and Patrick Macnee, and the script, "The Proteus Affair," was full of inside references to U.N.C.L.E. and THE AVENGERS. He also wrote for a short-lived Paramount series, THE RENEGADES. His trade paperback, THE BOOK OF KISSES, was published by Dembner Books/W.W. Norton and included material on THE MAN FROM U.N.C.L.E.

Robert Short has done special effects and miniature work for such motion pictures as E.T., STAR TREK—THE MOTION PICTURE, PIRANHA, 1941, CLOSE ENCOUNTERS OF THE THIRD KIND, ALLIGATOR, FIREFOX, BEETLEJUICE, COCOON: THE RETURN and the mermaid's tail in SPLASH. As a screenwriter he co-authored the story for the sf/horror film SCARED TO DEATH.

BRING BACK U.N.C.L.E.?

The story of their U.N.C.L.E. feature started in 1978 when Biederman and Short started talking about how great it would be if someone brought U.N.C.L.E. back as a motion picture, not unlike what was being done with STAR TREK. "Then we thought, well, why don't we do it?" Biederman recalled. "It was an idea we took very seriously right from the beginning."

It was less than two weeks before they got back together to discuss the ideas they'd come up with. They spent another two months working those ideas into a script. Then they began what would turn out to be a giant three and a half year effort to bring their dream to the silver screen. Why they didn't succeed is a story of how Hollywood works. . . or doesn't work.

Although it would be quite some time later before they learned differently, they believed that Norman Felton had a controlling interest in the property. Thus they figured that they had better go to him first because if he liked their project it would be easier to get it moving. And if he didn't like it, then it wouldn't be made at all. As it turned out, MGM actually owns 100 percent of U.N.C.L.E., and while Norman Felton would be a profit participant in any use of the U.N.C.L.E. property, he could not control how it was used.

After establishing contact with Felton through an agent, Biederman and Short were invited to his home. Felton, very open and amiable, talked about old times as well as other attempts to revive U.N.C.L.E. on some level which had come to naught. (One of these was the Goff and Roberts "The Malthusian Affair.") He had even tried to go the independent financing route to get an U.N.C.L.E. movie made at one point, but that had fallen by the wayside. Felton was enthusiastic at the meeting with Biederman and Short and suggested they write down their ideas, whereupon they handed him a copy of their script. Felton was very pleased just from paging through it and said, "Well, this is wonderful. Let me read it and I'll get back to you."

It was about a week later that they received the script back in the mail along with a two-page critique of it that Felton had written. "After Norman Felton's initial critique of our script, Bob and I hammered out a rewrite in two week's time that incorporated some of Norman's suggestions. . . but only those we were willing to live with without compromising the integrity of U.N.C.L.E.," Biederman recalled.

A TONED DOWN U.N.C.L.E.?

Some of the criticisms Felton made had to do with things that Biederman and Short believed were very much a part of the U.N.C.L.E. mythos. "I think he felt that there was too much violence in our script," Biederman explained, "and yet it was no more 'action oriented' than the series was. Norman always substitutes sleep darts for bullets. He's squeamish about the effects on people, especially the young, when it comes to violence, even in our kind of fantasy.

"I remember that when I was a kid, back in the sixties, I wrote Norman a ten page letter raving about U.N.C.L.E., and he wrote back saying "U.N.C.L.E. has disbanded now. They don't use guns any more and they're all for peace." But as far as we were concerned, they did use sleep darts—we just didn't go out of our way every single time to say so.

"There's one point in our script where we have an aerial battle with jets and Solo has to break some glass and fire at the other plane. Well, he couldn't very well use sleep darts, and in actuality U.N.C.L.E. did use bullets on occasion. Their guns took different kinds of ammunition. But Norman was really touchy about that. He also didn't think our basic plot was credible—taking over the world through economic means. Norman found this concept dull, whereas we thought it was very exciting and much better than having them up against another super-weapon,

"But he did say that our feelings for the principal U.N.C.L.E. characters was very good and that not many writers on the series could match us in how well we knew Solo and Illya. On the other hand he felt that perhaps we were being a bit too witty in the script, with which we did not agree. There was a lot of humor in the series, especially the banter between Solo and Illya. We felt that one of the key things about U.N.C.L.E. that made it stand out was the character interplay and we thought we had just the right amount of humor.

"Norman also felt we used too many of the old gadgets. But we did update them. Instead of the pen communicator, we had a little calculator card, and that was before this sort of idea proliferated. We had a card so they could check in U.N.C.L.E. headquarters and immediately tie into the computer in order to get data, instead of the way it used to be with Waverly saying, 'We'll feed this information in and get back to you.' So we kept some things and didn't keep others."

THE DIRECT APPROACH

It was following their contact with Norman Felton that the duo made the first of what would be many contacts with MGM Studios over their revival plans.

Biederman's agent arranged a meeting with Mark Canton, an executive who is no longer with the studio. But when the two writers showed up for the scheduled meeting, a secretary sheepishly informed them that Canton had split early to attend the Oscar presentation that night. The meeting was rescheduled and proved to be no more enjoyable than being stood up had been.

"It was very pressured and very brief. He didn't want to spend much time and just asked us to tell him the idea." Canton explained to them that the studio had considered similar proposals over the years, and asked if they pictured Vaughn and McCallum as redoing their old roles because Canton felt that was secondary and "you could get any actors in these roles." Biederman and Short were stunned at the idea that MGM could consider U.N.C.L.E. without Vaughn and McCallum. Canton ended the meeting abruptly, took the script, and within two weeks had returned it saying that MGM wasn't interested in doing something like that at the moment.

But just because one person at a studio says no, doesn't mean that it's the end of a dream. Studio regimes come and go with dizzying regularity in Hollywood—so much so that it seems as if offices should be equipped with revolving doors. So Biederman and Short watched and waited and kept resubmitting to MGM whenever the time was right.

One of the regimes they submitted the project to expressed the opinion that you couldn't compete with James Bond, and that this was one of the key reasons that MGM did not want to do an U.N.C.L.E. theatrical feature. They saw it as a Bond-like property and felt that Bond had the market cornered for that type of film. This was before the corporate link-up between MGM and United Artists into the entity now known as MGM/UA.

U.N.C.L.E. VS. BOND

But the writers felt that U.N.C.L.E. was very different from Bond, and that espionage thrillers were a wide-open genre, just as science fiction is. Biederman wrote them a lengthy argument in a letter which said in effect, "Look, are you saying a studio should not have made ALIEN because STAR TREK has the market covered?" MGM remained unpersuaded.

Then the personnel changed once more and the writers had a meeting with Mike Nathenson and Madelyn Warren. While Mike was enthusiastic to their proposal, Warren just sat listening. They left the script with him on a high note, but it came back from Madelyn Warren who said that while the feature division wasn't interested in it that she believed there might be some interest in the television division as a TV movie.

They got back to Mike Nathenson, who continued to express interest and said that he would not only get back to them, but that he would try to guarantee that Biederman and Short would be the pivotal force behind the project, or at the very least be definitely involved should MGM decide to proceed with it.

"And that brings me to one point about the project that was very dangerous because there was actually no guarantee that somebody wouldn't say, 'Well, we'll just do it ourselves; goodbye,' because we didn't own the rights, MGM did, and so there was that risk," Biederman explained. "We had some attorneys in on it from the begin-

ning and they warned us right-
ly that this could happen. So
that was a risk from the beginning, and from what we heard
from Norman, MGM was not
going to talk about giving up
any rights so that somebody
else could film it. We didn't
even try that route after everything that Norman had tried.
This was the risk we were taking."

YET ANOTHER DIRECT APPROACH

So the script entered the
infrastructure of MGM once
more and when Mike got back
to the authors he stated that
what the project needed to get
a go signal from MGM was a
firm commitment from Robert
Vaughn, David McCallum and
a television network that wanted to air it. For whatever reason, Mike wanted the two
authors to pursue Vaughn and
McCallum. They went through
attorneys to contact the two
actors, who agreed separately.

"We were thrilled,"
Biederman commented. "We
had Vaughn and McCallum."
What made this an even bigger
relief is that it had been an
unspoken fear that should the
two actors not want to be
involved, U.N.C.L.E. would be
dead as far as they were con-

cerned. So this good news
meant that another major hur-
dle had been overcome.

Mike Nathenson was sur-
prised and pleased and said
that he'd get back to the people
in charge of MGM television
and take it from there. Several
weeks passed and then the
writers heard that for unknown
reasons the interest at MGM TV
had cooled, but Mike also said
that if the interest reheated
he'd let the authors know.

"But we decided not to
wait," said Biederman. Their
enthusiasm was still undamp-
ened. "We thought about the
feature ideas again because
we'd always wanted to do it as
a feature, much more than as a
TV movie. We wondered, now
that we had Vaughn and
McCallum, if that would make
any difference. So we got back
to Madelyn Warren over in features and I asked her this. She
said she would reconsider the
project if we packaged it."

A YEAR LONG ORGANIZATION

To fully package the project
took another year. Many names
were considered for each role
in the script and it took an
average of two months to get
answers from people by the
time it got through their agents

and then to the talent and back again, and then through phone calls and so on. Then if they got a rejection from one of their choices, that was two months lost and it had to go out to someone else.

They tried getting as many of the original U.N.C.L.E. alumni as possible. Their first choice for director was Richard Donner, who had been a director on the old series. "We thought he'd be perfect because he'd also be a bankable name that would help get this picture going and off the ground." But after months, they still hadn't gotten an answer from him. They made endless trips to his office and always just missed him. Even sitting outside his office all day in a car didn't work. Finally they discovered his home address and went to his house, where they found him with his manager. While Donner was enthusiastic about the idea, he couldn't even give a tentative commitment because he was just beginning production on LADYHAWKE. But Donner recommended Boris Sagal, who had directed a fourth season U.N.C.L.E. episode.

"I called Boris and talked to him, and he expressed interest, saying that when we had a go-ahead on the project to call him," Biederman revealed.

Then a few weeks later, on May 22, 1981, Boris Sagal was killed when he accidentally walked into a moving tail rotor of a helicopter he had just stepped out of while scouting locations for the TV movie WORLD WAR III. A new director had to be found. Buzz Kulik was recommended, but he was busy with another project.

"Bob and I also met with Peter Hyams, just after the release of OUTLAND. He read our script but we ultimately had creative differences on how we envisioned the movie. Peter did not want Vaughn or McCallum in the film; he felt Napoleon Solo should be played by Tom Selleck. Bob and I could not go for such an approach."

DIRECTORS AND ACTORS

Another director whom they tried for was Richard Rush, "because one of my favorite films is THE STUNT MAN. I thought it was wonderful, and such a good action movie, and the way it dealt with the fine line between reality and fantasy was also, I think, a good part of U.N.C.L.E." But again, Rush was already committed to something else.

Eventually they did get Arthur Hiller, director of SILVER STREAK. Unlike Peter Hyams, he would only agree to do the film after being assured that they did indeed have interest from Vaughn and McCallum in reprising their roles for the film.

For the female lead they approached Sally Field, Mary Steenburgen and a few others before getting a commitment from Jane Seymour. Then, when they'd had the package assembled and were promoting Seymour, someone from her agent's office called demanding to know what was going on and denying knowledge of her commitment. Short and Biederman produced documentation to prove that they had received a positive response from that office, but apparently somewhere along the way someone in the agency had reversed the decision.

To play the role of the main villain, Klaus Kinski was cast (though Donald Sutherland had also been considered). He happened to be at MGM studios at that time, working on BUDDY, BUDDY with Jack Lemmon. His agent forwarded him the script and he expressed definite interest in playing the role of Kalfon Amherst.

INTERNATIONAL STAR

As the villainess, Serena, Laura Antonelli was definitely committed. The part had also been offered to Catherine Deneuve and Marthe Keller. Biederman discussed the project with Laura via her agent in Rome. A member of the Italian Consulate stationed in Los Angeles, Vincenzo Cataldo, served as intermediary by personally delivering the script to Laura's agent in Rome. The agent passed along the script to Laura, who was very interested in the part. Apart from further salary negotiations, the only request that she had was that there should be a standby American/Italian translator on the set during the shooting of her scenes once the feature film went into production. Though she could speak English, it was somewhat rusty. THE MAN FROM U.N.C.L.E. would have been her first American movie.

They also contacted Ringo Starr in England for what would have been a wonderful bit-part—the role of a THRUSH-controlled billionaire corporate executive. One of the "hooks" to get him interested was the offering of the part of Serena to his wife, Barbara Bach, thereby giving them a husband and wife teaming in the film. But Laura Antonelli came through first for her role.

"We tried contacting Jerry Goldsmith," Biederman said, "because he had done the original U.N.C.L.E. theme, but we had difficulty reaching him because he was out of the country a lot. We were never able to talk to him and only reached his agent, who said that Jerry wouldn't want to go back to anything old, so we really don't know if Jerry would have been interested or not."

However, they did sign up Gerald Fried, who had done a tremendous amount of scoring for the original series, and who later went on to score THE RETURN OF THE MAN FROM U.N.C.L.E. "Bob and I particularly liked his style on the show, and felt he would be ideal to do the feature. Also, Fried had since won an Emmy for his score of the TV mini-series ROOTS, so he would be fairly bankable as a composer in our package."

MORE MEETINGS AND CONTACTS

Another key element was Ken Adam. He had been the production designer on many of the James Bond movies, including GOLDFINGER.

"After reading our script he graciously told us that it was 'better than most of the Bond scripts' he'd read. He agreed to join us, pending his availability at the time we were ready to begin. Ken even went out of his way to drop me notes notifying me of where he could be found when he switched studios to work on a new picture."

Bob and Danny met personally with Fred Koenekamp, who was the cinematographer on the entire U.N.C.L.E. series. "Like Donner, he was now a major talent in features, and consequently ideal for our project. We met with him on the set of FIRST MONDAY IN OCTOBER, on which he was serving as director of photography. Fred recounted all the old days of working on U.N.C.L.E.—how he would light scenes by merely throwing lights at cave and hallway walls. It was great fun for him, he said. He remembered that Vaughn was always so studious, rushing off after every scene to study for his USC PhD exams. We told Fred about the feature film revival and he was extremely enthusiastic about the project. He also felt that Richard Donner was an ideal choice for director—Donner was still in the running at that point in time."

THE PRESENTA-TION PACKAGE

After a year of hard work, their package was completed. It was now time to assemble the visual elements that would be used in their presentation to MGM. These included:

1) A snappy-looking fold-out brochure which featured their full talent package (including credits and a photo of each individual), brief descriptions of both the U.N.C.L.E. property and the revival's storyline, plus artwork dramatizing the proposed project.

2) A color presentation booklet containing projected sales pitch, development proposal, background on the series' popularity and success, a statistic look at TV revivals utilizing a large ratings/box office chart, surveys on box office appeal based on age range and theater attendance, a studying of merchandising potential, a seventeen page story synopsis, plus photos and bios on their package talent and how each element fitted into the U.N.C.L.E. feature.

3) A three-quarter inch video cassette which they produced gave a capsulized visual review of the original TV series, plus current footage of their principal cast members. They had learned that some people needed a refresher on U.N.C.L.E., and most wanted to see how Vaughn and McCallum looked these many years later.

4) Large photo presentation boards on the cast and crew, plus artists' renderings of several key sets designed for the film.

5) The script.

THANKS BUT NO THANKS

Frank Marshall was working on the MGM lot at the time, busy with producer chores on three Steven Spielberg projects: RAIDERS OF THE LOST ARK, POLTERGEIST and E.T., so Biederman and Short secured an introduction, presented Marshall with their package and invited him to join it as executive producer. Marshall was enthusiastic with the project and gave a tentative agreement, pending the timing of an MGM go-ahead on U.N.C.L.E. and his own responsibilities to Spielberg. In the meantime he served as a consultant to the men during their creation of an MGM proposal, advising them primarily on budgetary and development matters.

"Then came the time we were ready to present everything and I called up Madelyn Warren, and she didn't even want to have a meeting with me!" Biederman angrily recalled. "I was floored! Finally she just said, 'Tell me what you have; I'm really busy.' I was really on the line because I didn't want to alienate her so I told her the key star names and she wrote them down and said she'd talk to David Chassman and get back to me as soon as possible."

As disappointed as they were about this cool reception, they decided to give it their best shot anyway. They assembled all of their visual aids and delivered them immediately to Madelyn's office, thereby giving her the option to use them in her own meeting with Chassman.

"Eventually we heard back from her. She called and talked to me for quite awhile and explained that they really weren't interested and that was it. It didn't seem that the package itself, as powerful as I believe it was, was persuasive enough. The bottom line was that MGM simply did not want to make U.N.C.L.E. into a movie, no matter what."

THE SPIELBERG CONNECTION

Well, not exactly. Sandy Climan, an executive assistant to studio topper Chassman, later admitted that involvement of someone like Spielberg or Warren Beatty would change MGM's mind. Of course any project can get made if it has Spielberg, Lucas or any of a small handful of similar top talent behind it. That's the way it works in Hollywood.

"Norman Felton had told us early on," Biederman commented, "that Spielberg as a young, aspiring filmmaker had once tried to sell an U.N.C.L.E. script to Norman during the run of the original series. The script wasn't bought, but this bit of trivia told us that an U.N.C.L.E. fan probably exists somewhere deep inside Steven Spielberg. It behooved us to contact him."

Short, an effects veteran on 1941, called Spielberg and invited him to direct the feature film. There was no positive response. "We assumed he wasn't interested in resurrecting an old hit series as a feature film," Biederman stated, "but we knew that wasn't true when a month or two later he announced plans for TWILIGHT ZONE—THE MOVIE."

Still not disillusioned, the two U.N.C.L.E. producer/writers conferred with Frank Marshall again, who felt that the project need not die just because of Warren's disinterest. He gathered up the visuals and went in to make his own presentation to another high-powered MGM executive, Willie Hunt. The project was once again in the hopper when there was a major announcement that rattled the lot: MGM would be merging with United Artists. Needless to say, this was distracting to the entire MGM brass, Hunt included. It was also at this time that Natalie Wood met with her tragic death during production of BRAINSTORM, a film being overseen by none other than Willie Hunt. Consequently, a fast response to Marshall's U.N.C.L.E. pitch was not forthcoming. Death and studio politics had intervened.

SOMEONE ELSE IS DOING IT?

While MGM shook, and Biederman and Short waited, curious rumors spread that a two-part MAN FROM U.N.C.L.E. episode, "The Five Daughters Affair," had been screened on the lot. Who would be running it, and why?

They learned that Ron Taylor in the television division had been at the screening, so they arranged a meeting with him to make sure that he was aware that they had a project under consideration as a feature, and that Mike Nathenson was covering for them in TV should that division warm up to the idea again. Ron explained that he had just joined MGM/UA and that a made-for-TV U.N.C.L.E. film was already on the books when he came in.

Biederman and Short had even met with Sam Rolfe and gotten his support to try and resurrect "The Malthusian Affair" in the event that they found moods had changed at MGM-TV. Rolfe was under contract elsewhere but felt certain that if they could revive the script, they would be able to do any rewrites and produce it themselves. The news of the impending TV movie came as both a surprise and a blow.

"We explained that for years we'd been trying to get this off the ground. He said, 'Don't stop your feature ideas. I think it sounds great and this doesn't mean that you have to abandon those plans. Keep plugging away.'"

Part of the confusion had resulted when Mike Nathenson had left MGM for UA, but with the merger he was back on the lot. Biederman contacted him and "he understood our position and that we had put in a lot of work and that we had a great deal of affection for the project, but he didn't want to talk about it. I think that he didn't want to acknowledge that he recalled his promises to us or to admit that he was responsible in any way for us being side-stepped. But we didn't hold him responsible. Something had just slipped up, despite our best efforts."

TELEVISION REVIVAL

They learned that Michael Sloan was the writer/director behind the U.N.C.L.E. TV movie, but when they attempted to contact him, Sloan would not return their calls. "While Bob and I were both interested in pooling our efforts, I don't think that Mike Sloan was interested in becoming involved with us. I personally feel that he saw us more as a threat. He'd read the articles about us doing an U.N.C.L.E. feature and I think that it was more of a competitive thing, whereas we were willing to join up in some way."

The fact that Sloan had an established track record in TV from having worked with Glen Larson on such shows as B.J. & THE BEAR apparently made his position more viable in the short run. Bob Short managed to establish contact with Sloan, and, based on his credits in doing special effects work on major films, was able to secure a spot in the proposed production as Technical Advisor.

"I think Bob put himself in a conflict-of-interest situation," Biederman commented. "He began throwing more and more of his support to Sloan, whereas it was apparent to me that Sloan had not yet even secured a deal. I was not anxious to walk away from three or four years of work on a major feature based on a TV producer's assurances to my partner that his TV movie was a sure thing."

As it turned out, it wasn't a sure thing at all; MGM TV reportedly had a problem with Sloan's budget. Biederman, meanwhile, pursued the feature film, even in the face of veiled threats from Sloan and angry phone calls from MGM TV. "A studio vice-president called me one afternoon. He was enraged about reports in the trades about the U.N.C.L.E. feature. Of course, the reports were all true. Yet this fellow was ordering me to stop what I was doing because ICM had already put Sloan, Vaughn and McCallum into a TV package from MGM.

I remember thinking, 'You call that a package?! I not only have Vaughn and McCallum, but a major line-up of award-winning international talent both in front of and behind the camera.' To this day my biggest regret is that I didn't say that to his face and use our package in an offensive maneuver against them. I decided to play it safe—cool and diplomatic. Of course, I held my ground regarding the feature. The VP claimed not to have known about it and apologized—but insisted the TV movie would prevail."

VIACOM CONNECTION

Talks between MGM and Sloan, however, finally broke down. Willie Hunt, meanwhile, sided with Madelyn Warren's verdict, in spite of Frank Marshall's backing. "The final option," Biederman explained, "was to try and make a deal with MGM to get the rights, in spite of Norman Felton's early admonitions." With Bob Short now in the Sloan stable, Biederman devised a complex formula which he hoped would set the groundwork for a deal

that MGM would accept. But he was still amazed when they bit.

"I was truly in awe at what I'd pulled off. Metro was ready to talk about selling me THE MAN FROM U.N.C.L.E." What put a damper on the news was an enthusiastic phone call from Short informing Biederman that Sloan was now doing the very same thing. Sloan secured the rights fast, for Viacom, a company that he'd just signed on with. Bob Short went to work for Sloan, as a labor of love, just to be involved with an U.N.C.L.E. film.

MGM continued to discuss feature rights with Biederman, though it seemed impractical to pursue in the face of an imminent TV movie. Curiously, Sloan not only employed (for obvious reasons) Vaughn and McCallum, but also several others from the Biederman-Short package: cinematographer Fred Koenekamp and composer Gerald Fried. After the filming of the TV movie was complete, Robert Vaughn phoned Biederman and expressed his continued interest in the feature film.

"With Bob Short and I sort of having gone our separate ways," Biederman noted, "I developed a new script, subtitled 'The Deadly Holiday Affair.' I engaged new attorneys, discussed my proposed rights deal with MGM, talked to Sam Rolfe about the possibility of his producing, and explored various avenues of financing. But when 'The Fifteen Years Later Affair' aired, everything came to a halt. That TV movie was everything I'd been trying to convince MGM that U.N.C.L.E. was not. It was, in my opinion, a very misguided attempt to revive the series and may well have buried the show forever. My spirit was killed by it and, by mere virtue of its existence, it damaged potential financing possibilities for future efforts, including both feature and concepts."

"THE 15 YEARS LATER AFFAIR"

Biederman found several important differences between his take on U.N.C.L.E. and the way the 1983 television movie treated the characters.

"The TV movie played up the issue of Solo's age, much the way Jay Bernstein handled West and Artie in WILD WILD WEST REVISITED; the rusty, older, out-of-shape hero who must get back in the saddle to fight his old cronies," Biederman observed. "I didn't care for that in either movie.

Ours would've been closer to the STAR TREK film. We'd planned to re-introduce our heroes as heroes, still top U.N.C.L.E. agents, older, wiser, but in tip-top shape. And I do believe Bob Vaughn could indeed have pulled that off. At his age, he can be pushed one way or the other. The movie-of-the-week pushed him toward 'old.' We'd have played up the vitality, wanting the big-screen audience to cheer at seeing a fondly-remembered hero back again as suave, cool and able as ever!"

Biederman also felt that the TV movie format was very limiting when compared to the capabilities of a theatrical production.

"A big-screen motion picture would give U.N.C.L.E. an epic proportion comparable to its image in our memories. A dimensional, exciting score (another weak area of the movie of the week). Swift, well-paced direction. Sets that bring the old show's locales up to date—by all means retaining Del Floria's Tailor Shop (an area of agreement between ourselves and Norman—we both envisioned a new U.N.C.L.E. film beginning back at the Tailor Shop), and enlarging and refurbishing the HQ. In short, we were shooting for class."

Dan also felt that the character interplay in THE RETURN OF THE MAN FROM U.N.C.L.E. was ill-conceived. "Solo and Illya would without a doubt have been the focal point of our film. Interplay, banter, subtle humor were of key importance. After 15 years, Solo and Kuryakin should not have been brought together just to send them in separate directions," such as the TV movie did.

END OF THE LINE

Michael Sloan's plans to revive the series were turned down by CBS, who were disappointed by the TV movie's ratings. This also affected the possibility of Biederman finally getting a feature film onto the screen.

"On a personal level, I put four years into the U.N.C.L.E. feature, and I now have many other projects going. The possibility of my having a go at U.N.C.L.E. again isn't nil, but it's certainly way on the back burner. I have certain ideas about how I'd pursue it in the future—time will tell. My honest feeling is that I think that the chances are much smaller now because there has already been one. That satisfaction has been gotten and it steals the thunder from doing another one. Everyone has seen what Solo and Kuryakin are like now, whether they like it or not."

As it turned out, that feature project for THE MAN FROM U.N.C.L.E. never did get the green light. The script written by Biederman and Short has been adapted and condensed into a one-issue comic book story which is slated to be published by Millennium in issue #3 of their MAN FROM U.N.C.L.E. comic book, which will probably appear in early 1994. The story has been retitled "The End of the World Affair."

We've read about how Danny Biederman and Bob Short tried to get an U.N.C.L.E. theatrical feature off the ground, but what is the behind-the-scenes story on the actual making of THE RETURN OF THE MAN FROM U.N.C.L.E.? Bob Short reveals how and why he accepted the chance to work on a competing project.

Chapter Sixteen

THE FIFTEEN YEARS LATER AFFAIR

THE RETURN OF THE MAN FROM U.N.C.L.E. aired April 5, 1983. This TV movie revival had an interesting genesis as well as plans for things which never made it into the final film. Bob Short, who was in partnership with Danny Biederman on the attempt to get MGM to consider making an U.N.C.L.E. feature film, became involved with THE FIFTEEN YEARS LATER AFFAIR early on and he knows a lot about what went into the making of this film.

Michael Sloan, the writer/producer of THE RETURN OF THE MAN FROM U.N.C.L.E., got the idea for the project from an associate, Douglas Benton. Sloan had been writing and producing for Universal television when he began working with Benton, who had been one of the producers on the U.N.C.L.E. series in the '60s. Benton mentioned in passing that it would be great to bring back THE MAN FROM U.N.C.L.E. and Sloan agreed. The germ of the idea began there.

"Sloan went to MGM with the idea," Short explained, "and approached the TV department and they said that they'd be interested in it." Sloan then took a trip to England where he spent two weeks writing an U.N.C.L.E. teleplay. Before writing the script, he viewed "The Five Daughters Affair" at MGM in order to get a feel for the show. This is how Bob Short discovered that there was a competing project in the works.

"During a meeting that I was having over at MGM, I heard from one of the security guards that an U.N.C.L.E. episode had just been run at the studio theater for a producer that was developing a film, and that was the first that I had heard of it," Short recalled. Then he made it a point to find out more about that project. Since Bob was known to people in the prop department from his collecting of the original props from the show, Bob Short was recommended to MGM as a technical consultant for the film.

The Michael Sloan script was then at MGM for several months being worked over to determine the budget, at the end of which time the studio declared that they couldn't do it because the budget would be too high. Sloan then decided to take the project to Viacom, whom he now had a working relationship with. Since CBS had already stated that they wanted to show the U.N.C.L.E. film were it to be made, Viacom decided that it would be worth their while to produce it.

THE NEW U.N.C.L.E.

"When it changed from being the MGM MAN FROM U.N.C.L.E. into the Viacom MAN FROM U.N.C.L.E., it began to shift into the new identity," Bob explained. "Anything that was new about the show is when it went over to Viacom, as far as the change of insignia, etc."

One of the reasons that MGM had deemed the project as being too expensive for them was because Sloan's script was very ambitious visually; certainly more ambitious than what was eventually filmed. "The original script was going to strive for a lot more," Short revealed. "Take for example the beginning of RETURN where the THRUSH operative in the Mojave desert shack sends up a jamming beacon and the plane carrying the H-bomb crashes off screen in the desert. Then there's just a close-up of the bomb and that's the way it looks in the show."

But in the original script the bomber was flying over the polar icecap and a completely different scene had been envisioned.

"This dome comes out of the snow, antennas poke out of it, the jet goes out of control and crashes. Then a Walker (a la STAR WARS) with a big THRUSH insignia on the side comes lurching out of the snow and walks over to the plane and gobbles the whole plane up in its belly and walks off. That was going to be the introduction of THRUSH. Obviously you can see the difference on how it was originally planned and how it devolved into a TV movie on a strictly TV budget," Bob observed.

LOCATION DEMANDS

In the original version of the script the headquarters of THRUSH was going to be like Piz Gloria, the mountaintop structure used by Blofeld in the movie ON HER MAJESTY'S SECRET SERVICE, including a helicopter raid which would have been similar to what was seen in that film.

"That was replaced with Hoover dam, and they had eighteen days to shoot the show and it all had to be done in very strict locations," Bob stated. "They went to Las Vegas for the first week of shooting and tried to squeeze as much as they could out of all the locations." Then after that they came back to Los Angeles and had to shoot in a two block radius of downtown L.A. where everything they'd be filming would be in walking distance.

"So within that two blocks they had to find the best thing that looked like an old hotel, a New York street, a building which pre-existed with an interior that kind of looked like U.N.C.L.E. headquarters, and that includes the hallways, Raleigh's office and the U.N.C.L.E. testing lab." And all of that had to be pretty much on the same block. "So you can see what kind of logistical problems there were to create the look of U.N.C.L.E., but without being able to sit down and spend the money on building an U.N.C.L.E. headquarters corridor or something like that. And we also had to find a tailor shop interior in that same area that could double for Del Floria's. So you can see how difficult something like that was to put together."

RESEARCH—WITH RESTRICTIONS

Bob Short joined the project when it was still in the development stages at MGM. In general his duties at that point were to keep an eye on preproduction and see that nothing went really outside the realm of U.N.C.L.E. and to give advice to the art director and the prop men and wardrobe as to what was within the realm of the U.N.C.L.E. venue.

"It was my responsibility to choose the episodes for everybody to watch to get a feel for the show. The edict from the top was that they had to be color episodes; nobody wanted to watch black and white. So I was not able to use first season as something to go by. Not even for research purposes. They didn't want to know about first season. So there was no first season referencing done whatsoever. So that was part of it. Checking on costumes."

Originally they were going to have everybody in jumpsuits because it was going to be easy to get a lot of them, and the two choices they had were orange and blue. At one point they almost had the U.N.C.L.E. agents in blue jumpsuits with black berets but Bob Short was able to talk them out of the beret which went to the THRUSH agents instead.

THE NEW LOOK

"Once preproduction (on the Viacom version) got going, they wanted a new U.N.C.L.E. insignia, so I cooked up one on my own and brought it in," Bob revealed. "And I suggested that they have an U.N.C.L.E. gun made since that was kind of the trademark of the old show, but nobody really wanted to spend the money on getting a new U.N.C.L.E. gun. I took it upon myself to basically have the U.N.C.L.E. gun done and brought it in. Then it got written into the script.

"There's a scene in the armory where they're being given new U.N.C.L.E. specials," Bob continued. "They go, 'Where are our old U.N.C.L.E. guns?' And 'Z' goes, they're in the Smithsonian but we've updated them and here are your new guns. I'm sure that you'll find them at first a little difficult to use.' Solo and Illya look at each other, and Solo reaches down and takes all the attachments, whips the gun together in a couple of seconds, throws it to Illya and Illya disassembles it and puts it back in the case in a matter of seconds. And 'Z' gives them this kind of 'smartass' kind of look." But all that's cut out.

"I had one of the original communicators from the show and I had Dave Heilman and Bruce Wegman down in San Diego duplicate it. Then during the shooting I was out there on a daily basis just to keep an eye on U.N.C.L.E. continuity, as it were, such as pronunciation of names and adding little touches here and there and just making sure that they weren't missing some of the U.N.C.L.E. universe stuff."

CONTINUITY

One of the arguments Bob lost was when he tried to explain why Solo and Illya wouldn't wear their U.N.C.L.E. badges outside of U.N.C.L.E. headquarters, but they told him that "this is the new U.N.C.L.E." and they did things differently now.

"I also suggested that when agents identify themselves inside U.N.C.L.E. headquarters that it might be interesting if they specify what section they're in. And then in post-production I was helping out with paperwork and making suggestions on music. I suggested Gerald Fried over Mike Post and things like that. Michael (Sloan) was really the person who made all the final decisions, but I basically found myself in a position where I could at least make some good recommendations to keep the universe intact. It was my job to go to MGM and track down the original tape of the sound effect for the communicator. For the title sequence I went back to MGM and dug up the original background plate of the continent that was used behind the original U.N.C.L.E. insignia on the old TV show."

The new insignias were done because Viacom felt that since they were doing a new show they wanted to have an updated look. This included updating the symbol of THRUSH from a small bird to a lightning bolt symbol. And yet the old THRUSH symbol does make a brief appearance in the TV movie.

NEW THRUSH AND OLD

"In the script it always refers to THRUSH as having a new lightning bolt insignia and it was in the script that the note that they get from Sepheran has a delicate thrush drawn at the bottom, and that was the only reference to a drawn thrush anywhere in the script," Bob explained. "And of course you never see the note on the screen so you don't know what it is. But there is a scene where Sepheran is drawing a thrush because he is being interrogated by Kowalski. And because Anthony Zerbe can't draw, for the prop department I drew half of the bird and then put a little dot outline for Anthony to fill in while he was doing that scene. So what I did, of course, is draw the original THRUSH insignia bird on the pad of paper and there's a very quick side shot of him holding the bird up and saying, 'This is the only thrush I know of,' and Kowalski is so dense he doesn't catch the fact that Sepheran has actually drawn the THRUSH insignia bird without the triangle around it. So those are the little things that I would continually try to throw in."

Also, although it isn't clear, if you look very carefully you can see an old style THRUSH insignia on the front of Sepheran's desk. He's old guard THRUSH so he's got the old insignia.

"I gave it to the prop department and said, 'Here,

slap this on the front of his desk as Sephran's personal insignia.' And of course people on the set would go, 'Why does he have a bird on his desk?' So even though the script called for a new lightning bolt style, I tried to stick in the old THRUSH insignia where I could."

THE FLASHBACK WE NEVER SAW

The most crucial scene which would have been filled with classic U.N.C.L.E. visual reference points was in the script and on the slate to be filmed, but was ultimately cut from the schedule due to time constraints.

"In the show, Illya has quit and they refer to Janus having double-crossed him, but you never really get a backstory on it. In the original script, and in the script that we were using during shooting, there was always a flashback sequence where Illya and a girl in a Soviet block nation are running from THRUSH agents. David was going to run with a black turtleneck on and his old shoulder holster with the old U.N.C.L.E. pistol, and the THRUSH agents were going to be dressed in the old THRUSH uniforms and have the old THRUSH rifles.

"The scene was going to be Illya running through the forest with this girl, THRUSH agents following and getting to this area that Janus is supposed to be at. Janus was going to be in the old U.N.C.L.E. car and the U.N.C.L.E. car drives off and leaves them there. The girl gets shot and killed and then it was going to fade to McCallum walking down the old U.N.C.L.E. corridor and we were going to rebuild one half section of Waverly's office and use the original table from Waverly's office and use stock footage of Leo G. Carroll looking up from his desk as David takes off his shoulder holster and slams it across the table and does kind of a PRISONER-esque sequence and bangs his fist on the table and walks out."

That was the last thing they were going to shoot, but they ran out of time. That was going to be the blast from the past. For the scene when Illya quits, Bob Short had to go through all of the U.N.C.L.E. episodes and find stock footage of the exterior of Del Floria's tailor shop for when Solo walks in. He had to find that without any cars in the shot which would have told what vintage the scene was. Then he also had to come up with footage that would tie in for that sequence of Waverly looking exactly in the right spot.

CHARACTER QUESTIONS

Although the flashback sequence related what drove Illya to quit working for U.N.C.L.E., nothing ever established why Napoleon Solo quit as well, and Bob Short admits that there never was any explanation concocted.

"The concept was basically that Michael (Sloan) wanted to do a revival where he arbitrarily decided that they both left U.N.C.L.E. for different reasons, and they're off doing different things when they are called back in. It was just an arbitrary decision on Michael's part.

Michael originally had Napoleon with the high fashion dress salon and Illya was the owner of the highly successful computer company. When he read the script, David McCallum told Michael that it would be much more interesting if he switched professions around. That's how Illya became the dress designer and Napoleon became the computer businessman, which is completely opposite where they

should have been." The switching of the careers is interesting in light of the sometimes observed fact that personality-wise, Robert Vaughn and David McCallum are each the opposite of the personas they portrayed on U.N.C.L.E., almost as though they borrow each other's personalities for their roles.

But regarding the fact that both of them had quit U.N.C.L.E., it could be argued that, yes, something could have happened to make Illya want to quit the organization but something really strange would have had to have happened for Napoleon Solo not to have become the head of U.N.C.L.E.

"But that's just a writer's choice," Short explained. "I had as much problem accepting Solo and Illya having left U.N.C.L.E. as I did THRUSH having been disbanded. THRUSH never seemed to me like the kind of organization that would be disbanded. It's too far-flung. One of the things they didn't want to deal with was the structure of THRUSH. In their own way they wanted to play it more like SPECTRE with a Blofeld-kind of character bringing this organization back together rather than have a THRUSH Central. A supreme council and ultimate computer was too weird for them, basically. It was too much for everybody to assimilate at the time."

LOST REFERENCES

It seems that in the decade since it originally aired that THE RETURN OF THE MAN FROM U.N.C.L.E. has fared pretty well with the fans. In retrospect it's something that's certainly not as bad as most of the third season episodes and there are some second season U.N.C.L.E. episodes which aren't even as coherent or as true to the U.N.C.L.E. format as RETURN OF THE MAN FROM U.N.C.L.E. was.

"One of the things that struck me as odd about the final film," Bob commented, "is that there was a lot more referencing to the style of the old show that was shot and was deleted in the editing, just for time's sake. What would happen was that the editor would look at the stuff, and it wasn't really dramatic stuff or things that needed to be in there, but they were definitely U.N.C.L.E. touches—and he deleted all that. Unfortunately a lot of U.N.C.L.E.-isms were lost such as when Solo goes into the new U.N.C.L.E. headquarters there's a whole sequence where Solo and Illya go into the toy

shop, go into the back room, and the sequence was shot so that it had sliding doors that open and they walk into a huge reception area with a lot of U.N.C.L.E. agents wandering back and forth and they are stopped at the reception area and given U.N.C.L.E. badges."

The director was going to have them walk up to the table, pick up the badges and put them on, but Bob Short explained that this would have been incorrect.

"No, they can't pick them up and put them on. The guy behind the desk has to touch them first and then give them to Solo and Illya because the chemicals on his fingertips have to activate the badges. So the guy had to touch the badges and hand them to Solo and Illya and they put them on and walk down the hallway. That sequence was completely cut out of the show because it was, 'who cares, they're just walking into a building and getting badges. No big deal. Cut it out.'

"There were things like that throughout," Bob adds, "that were U.N.C.L.E.-isms that they could live without because they had to tighten up the show. I was kind of miffed. There was also a museum in the armory room with old THRUSH rifles, but those shots were all left out."

INSIDE JOKES

There's more!

"There's an interesting scene where Solo comes down the mountainside and he gets to the bottom of the mountain and jumps into a truck. He then takes out the U.N.C.L.E. gun and puts it together on camera, which the old show used to do in close-ups."

There were also a lot of other references which were deleted from the script. There were references to THE AVENGERS (which had starred Patrick Macnee, who played Sir John Raleigh, the new head of U.N.C.L.E. in RETURN OF THE MAN FROM U.N.C.L.E.), as well as Dr. Who jokes. "There were a lot more tongue-in-cheek references to spy shows and science fiction shows that were sprinkled throughout the film," Bob explained. "It's funny. Simon Williams, who plays the Englishman they protect, in one of the scenes is wearing a little scarf. It's just a little throw-away that he's wearing a scarf.

In the script, and the way it was supposed to have been, was that the scarf is multi-colored and about five yards long and is very distinctively recognizable. And when Napoleon meets him he looks at the scarf and Simon looks at Napoleon and goes, 'A Dr. Who scarf, of course.' And it's like a running gag throughout the rest of the show, the fact that he's wearing the Tom Baker Dr. Who scarf. But the wardrobe department couldn't find a Dr. Who scarf, so that got axed.

"Also, when the note comes in from Sepheran, John Raleigh makes the comment, 'What's all this about? What's so important? Have the Daleks invaded?' There were pretty cute references throughout. Some of that was deleted from the script. I guess the director felt that was too kitchy. Slowly but surely those little references got deleted until there were none left, except for the Simon Williams character wearing a little scarf, and the genesis of that scarf was a heavy Dr. Who and the Daleks reference, but it never made it to the screen."

As Bob explained it, such deletions occurred due to the pressure the production was under to get made in a very short amount of time.

"Again it's part of that, 'We only got eighteen days to make the show. We only want what we need and we've got to just kind of trim it down.'"

HEADACHES

Then there was the matter of the prison scene, which was shot at an actual prison.

"We weren't allowed to wear bluejeans because that was the prison wardrobe. All the extras in the scene were real guards and real prisoners. One of the weird things that happened was the helicopter which the transportation guy had arranged for arrived and it was from 'Circus Circus' (the Las Vegas hotel/casino) and it was pink with balloons painted on it. Needless to say, it didn't quite fit the sinister THRUSH look, so they immediately had to scramble, go to a local airport and find another helicopter. So originally the THRUSH helicopter was almost a pink helicopter."

There was also a scene where Illya was supposed to use a hang glider to get into a THRUSH cave. But the night before the scene was going to be shot near Las Vegas, the hang glider was assembled and left outside where a wind came along during the night and ripped the hang glider to pieces. As an alternative they came up with the idea of Illya discovering that there is a secret entrance to the THRUSH cave through someone's backyard swimming pool.

There's a variety of reasons that certain things appeared in the film. For instance, George Lazenby as "J.B." was a character who was always in the script and he appeared in the film because he's an old friend of Michael Sloan's. Lazenby drove an Aston Martin which belongs to Bob Short, although all of the gimmicks it had on screen were products of the prop department.

WHY IT DIDN'T RETURN AGAIN

Although there were discussions about spinning RETURN OF THE MAN FROM U.N.C.L.E. into a new series, CBS didn't feel that the ratings were quite good enough, although it came closer than many fans realized.

"That was what's called a 'back-door pilot.' It was done as a TV movie, but it was also definitely done as a pilot that, if it had gotten better ratings would have gone to series."

There are two different levels of ratings. There are the overnight ratings, which come in the next day from certain key major cities, and then there's the actual ratings which figure in every part of the country.

"The overnights were through the roof and everybody figured we had a series on our hands. Then when the final ratings came in they were two points below going to series, and everybody was pretty upset about that, because everybody was really looking forward to it going to series."

For awhile Sam Rolfe (who died in 1993) and Norman Felton were trying to get another TV movie made based on their 1970's script "The Malthusian Affair" which would have featured two new U.N.C.L.E. agents working with Solo and Illya. The head of U.N.C.L.E. would have been a computer.

U.N.C.L.E. FOR THE 90S

A lot of things have happened with MGM and U.N.C.L.E. since the TV movie THE RETURN OF THE MAN FROM U.N.C.L.E. aired back in 1983. MGM's film library was acquired by Ted Turner, who for several years tried to put together some sort of U.N.C.L.E. revival film. Then in 1993 Davis Entertainment announced that they had acquired the right to make an U.N.C.L.E. motion picture, which at this point is still in the very earliest stages of development.

In light of the box office success of such motion picture revivals of TV shows like THE ADDAMS FAMILY and THE FUGITIVE, many other television revivals are in the works of which U.N.C.L.E. is merely one of many. What these modern revivals all have in common is that they have been completely recast with different, younger actors so that they could continue with several sequels if the popularity is there. Even the original cast of STAR TREK is being eased out to make way for the younger cast of THE NEXT GENERATION, and the LOST IN SPACE movie remake will recast with younger performers as well.

So THE MAN FROM U.N.C.L.E. is destined to return, and while it will undoubtedly recast the leading roles one can at least hope that much of the surrounding magic which made the original series so memorable and interesting will at least be retained to achieve the right atmosphere of intrigue and imagination.

PART TWO
The Stories

Chapter Seventeen
First Season

(Black and white)

Regulars
Napoleon Solo: Robert Vaughn
Ilya Kuryakin: David McCallum
Alexander Waverly: Leo G. Carroll

#1: "The Vulcan Affair"
(Original air date: 9/22/64)
Written by Sam Rolfe
Directed by Don Medford
GUEST CAST
Elaine May Donaldson: Patricia Crowley
Andrew Vulcan: Fritz Weaver

The adventures of Solo and Kuryakin get off to a rousing start when U.N.C.L.E.'s chief Waverly discovers the THRUSH scheme to kill an African potentate. (For more details see THE BIRTH OF U.N.C.L.E..)

#2: "The Iowa-Scuba Affair"
(9-29-64)
Written by Harold Jack Bloom
Directed by Richard Donner
GUEST CAST
Jill Dennison: Katherine Crawford
Clint Spinner: Slim Pickens

Latin Woman: Margart Cordova

An attempt on Solo's life is foiled, and his assailant, a soldier, is killed. The discovery of scuba gear concealed in the dead man's motorcycle leads to an investigation that uncovers a secret new plane with a deadly cargo

#3: "The Quadipartite Affair"
(10/6/64)
Written by Alan Caillou
Directed by Richard Donner
GUEST CAST
Marion Raven: Jill Ireland
Gervaise Ravel: Anne Francis
Adam Pattner: Richard Anderson
Horth: Roger C. Carmel

Introducing the beautiful but deadly Gervaise Ravel, a woman destined to trouble U.N.C.L.E. more than once.

#4: "The Shark Affair" (10/6/64)
Written by Alvin Sapinsley
Directed by Marc Daniels
GUEST CAST
Captain Shark: Robert Culp

Elsa Barnam: Sue Ann Langdon
Mr. MacInernay: James Doohan

Captain Shark is busy raiding ships on the high seas. A humane man, he sets everyone adrift in life rafts before sinking the ships. But his motivation seems strange: all he takes from his victims are powdered milk, shoelaces and aspirin.

The presence of James Doohan makes this episode of special interest to STAR TREK fans.

#5: "The Deadly Games Affair"
(10/20/64)
Written by Dick Nelson
Directed by Alvin Ganzer
GUEST CAST
Professor Amadeus: Alexander Scourby
Angelique: Janine Gray
Chuch Boskirk: Burt Brickerhoff
Terry Brent: Brooke Bundy

Professor Amadeus is the new name of a former Nazi scientist who is still working on his efforts to revive the dead. He is also a serious stamp collector, which gives U.N.C.L.E. a good idea how to get close to him. But when an innocent stamp collector gets in the way, it's another big adventure that leads to the unveiling of the Professor's plan to invent a technique for reviving the dead. Guess whose body is stashed in this loyal Nazi's garage?

#6: "The Green Opal Affair"
(10/27/64)
Written by Robert E. Thompson
Directed by John Peyser
GUEST CAST
Walter G. Brach: Carroll O'Connor
Chris Linnel: Joan O'Brien
Chuke: Shuji J. Nozawa
Dr. Stallmacher: Milton Seltzer

When a returning U.N.C.L.E. agent goes haywire, the code phrase "Green Opal" leads Solo and Ilya to the Pacific, and to wheelchair-bound financier Brach, who, with Dr. Shtallmacher, is heading the THRUSH plot to program people's minds.

#7: "The Gucco Piano Affair"
(11/10/64)
Written by Alan Caillou
Directed by Richard Donner
GUEST CAST
Raven: Jill Ireland
Ravel: Anne Francis
Bufferton: John Van Dreelen
Chess Player: Norman Felton
Texan: Sam Rolfe
Writer: Joseph Calvelli
Drunk: Richard Donner

As the sequel to "The Quadripartite Affair" opens, word arrives that arch-villainess Gervaise Ravel and her accomplice, Bufferton, have been located in Peru.

#8: "The Double Affair"
(11/17/64)
Written by Clyde Ware
Directed by John Newland
GUEST CAST
Serena: Senta Berger
Sandy Wister: Sharon Farrell

A Solo lookalike and murderous wind-up robot toys are but a few of the pitfalls in this adventure. (See also U.N.C.L.E. MOVIES)

#9: "The Project Strigas Affair"
(11/24/64)
Written by Henry Misrock
Directed by Joe Sargent
GUEST CAST
Mike Donfield: William Shatner
Anne Donfield: Peggy Ann Garner
Kurasov: Werner Klemperer
Vladek: Leonard Nimoy

Waverly decides that Ambassador Kurasov is becoming a threat to the West, so U.N.C.L.E. dupes him into believing in a fabricated military secret and enlists the aid of Mike and Ann Donfield, a young couple, in discrediting him.

Shatner and Nimoy worked together for the first time here.

#10: "The Finny Foot Affair"
(12/2/64)
Written by Jack Turley and Jay Simms
Directed by Marc Daniels
GUEST CAST

Chris Larson: Kurt Russell

An experimental chemical accidentally causes an entire Norwegian village to die of old age.

#11: "The Neptune Affair"
(12/8/64)
Written by John W. Bloch and Henry Sharp
Directed by Vincent McEveety
GUEST CAST
Felicia Lavimore: Marta Kristen

A threat to Russia's wheat crop threatens world peace; Ilya heads home, while Solo poses as a farmer. The sympathetic Felicia Lavimore is played by Marta Kristen, the future Judy Robinson of LOST IN SPACE.

#12: "The Dove Affair" (12/15/64)
Written by Robert Towne
Directed by John Peyser
GUEST CAST
Satine: Ricardo Montalban
Sarah Taub: June Lockhart

Solo must steal a medallion which contains the names of THRUSH agents— off a dead dictator's body as it lies in state! To get out of the country, which is overrun by THRUSH agents in key positions, Solo must trust the only honest man around: the head of the secret police.

#13: "The King of Knaves Affair"
(12/22/64)
Written by Ellis Marcus
Directed by Michael O'Herlihy
GUEST CAST
King Fazik: Paul Stevens
Ernestine Pepper: Diana Millay
Gema Lusso: Arlene Martel

When the world's crime bosses start disappearing, U.N.C.L.E. wants to know why— so Napoleon Solo poses as a master criminal.

#14: "The Terbuf Affair" (12/29/64)
Written by Alan Caillou
Directed by Richard Donner
GUEST CAST
Clara Valdar: Madlyn Rhue
Major Vicek: Albert Paulsen

Solo and Kuryakin take a vacation in a small European country— a cover for their mission to trace stolen foreign aid money.

#15: "The Deadly Decoy Affair"
(1/11/65)
Written by Albert Aley
Directed by Alvin Ganzer
GUEST CAST
Music: Walter Scharf

This episode sees Mr. Waverly in a rare field job— at one point he even goes hand-to-hand with a THRUSH killer!

#16: "The Fiddlesticks Affair"
(1/18/65)
Story by Aben Kandel
Teleplay by Peter A. Fields
Directed by Theodore J. Flicker
GUEST CAST
Marcel Rudolph: Dan O'Herlihy
Susan Callaway: Marlyn Mason

A tough job at a casino which conceals the THRUSH treasury leads Solo and Ilya to recruit the services of Marcel, a safecracker who wants to join THRUSH but who has been rejected.

#17: "The Yellow Scarf Affair"
(1/25/65)
Written by Robert Yale and Boris Ingster
Directed by Ron Winston
GUEST CAST
Dirdre Purbhani: Kamali Devi
Sita Chandhi: Neile Adams

The action here is in India, where an U.N.C.L.E. agent named McAllister picks up a typewriter case which actually contains a new code machine. But as McAllister flies back to New York, a group of Thuggees raid the plane and reclaim the device.

#18: "The Mad, Mad Tea Party Affair"
(2/1/65)
Written by Dick Nelson
Directed by Seymour Robbie
GUEST CAST

Mr. Hemmingway: Richard Haydn
Dr. Egret: Lee Meriwether

A pen that destroys the brain, and explosive ashtrays, add up to make this a truly deadly affair as the security of U.N.C.L.E. headquarters is penetrated and seemingly threatened prior to the visit of the President of the United States.

#19: "The Secret Scepter Affair"
(2/8/65)
Written by Anthony Spinner
Directed by Marc Daniels
GUEST CAST
Morgan: Gene Raymond
Aiz: Ziva Rodann

Our heroes freelance again in a Mid-East nation where Solo's old army colonel is fighting for democracy.

#20: "The Bow-Wow Affair"
(2/15/65)
Written by Alan Caillou
Directed by Sherman Marks
GUEST CAST
Guido Panzini: Pat Harrington, Jr.
QuentinLester Baldwin: Leo G. Carroll
Alice Baldwin: Susan Oliver

Financier Baldwin avoids a murder attempt out of sheer luck and alerts his cousin Waverly to the problem.

#21: "The Four Steps Affair"
(2/22/65)
Written by Peter A. Fields
Directed by Alvin Ganzer
GUEST CAST
Sarah: Lee Chapman
Miki: Michel Petit
Kelly Brown: Susan Seaforth

When an U.N.C.L.E. agent is betrayed to THRUSH by his girlfriend, he lives just long enough to alert Waverly to their latest plot: the takeover of the Himalayan nation of Shanti.

#22: "The See-Paris-And-Die Affair"
(3/1/65)
Written by Peter A. Fields and Sheldon Stark
Directed by Alf Kjellin
GUEST CAST
Max Van Schreeten: Lloyd Bochner
Mary Pilgrim: Kathryn Hays

The Von Schreeton brothers are both in love with would-be singer Mary Pilgrim, so they buy a Paris nightclub to advance her career. Since THRUSH and U.N.C.L.E. are both after diamonds stolen by the brothers, Mary becomes a pawn in their struggle. A visit to the Tomb of the Unknown Spy is a nice touch in this complicated storyline.

#23: "The Brain-Killer Affair"
(3/8/65)
Written by Archie L. Tegland

Directed by James Tegland
GUEST CAST
Dr. Agnes Dabree: Elsa Lanchester
Cecile Bergstrom: Yvonne Craig
Gabhail Samoy: Abraham Sofaer
Jason: Roosevelt Grier

A THRUSH agent slips a pill into Waverly's drink as he is out and about; the U.N.C.L.E. chief is rushed to the nearest hospital where, unfortunately, a pair of THRUSH doctors are waiting to experiment on Waverly! The whole organization of U.N.C.L.E. is thrown into disarray, but our heroes save the day. Waverly is never quite as helpless as he might seem.

#24: "The Hong Kong Shilling Affair" (3/15/65)
Written by Alan Caillou
Directed by Alvin Ganzer
GUEST CAST
Bernie Oren: Glen Corbett
Heavenly Cortelle: Karen Sharpe
Cleveland: Gavin McLeod
Merry: Richard Kiel
Jade: Mikio Taka

Vacationing in Hong Kong, American tourist Bernie Oren tries to help a lady in distress— only to get in the way of Solo and Ilya, who are after the notorious Heavenly Cortelle. All four characters become involved in a deadly plot which features the oversized villain Merry (Richard Kiel). Fortunately for all involved (except the bad guys),

Heavenly turns out to be an undercover agent of the Hong Kong police, and has been helping Solo and Ilya all along.

#25: "The Never-Never Affair" (3/22/65)
Written by Dean Hargrove
Directed by Joseph Sargent
GUEST CAST
Mandy: Barbara Feldon
Victor Gervais: Cesar Romero
Varner: John Stephenson

Victor Gervais, the head THRUSH agent in France, comes to New York in an attempt to retrieve some important information. Barbara Feldon's first espionage adventure. Soon she would be starring as Agent 99 on the U.N.C.L.E. parody GET SMART.

#26: "The Love Affair" (3/29/65)
Written by Albert Aley
Directed by Marc Daniels
GUEST CAST
Brother Love: Eddie Albert
Pearl Rolfe: Maggie Pierce
Dr. Janos Hradny: Robert Harris
Magda: Tracey Roberts

Evangelist Brother Love holds the key to the death of a famous scientist who has invented a new missile guidance system. Love wants the plans so that he can rule the world from his own orbiting platform.

Love's gospel is a front for his hunger for power and money. As so often befalls villains on this show, Love is blown up with the bomb which he had intended for our intrepid heroes.

#27: "The Gazebo In The Maze Affair" (4/6/65)
Written by Dean Hargrove and Anthony Ellis
Directed by Alf Kjellin
GUEST CAST
Partridge: George Sanders
Edith Partridge: Jeanette Nolan
Jenkins: John Alderson
Forrest: John Orchard
Peggy: Donnie Franklin

A London bus on the streets of New York carries an abducted Ilya to the private domain of the eccentric Mr. Partridge, a man who wants to live in the past, and apparently wants the rest of the world to join him there. Ilya is a pawn in Partridge's plan to abduct Mr. Waverly. When Solo goes to rescue Ilya, he discovers that behind every great (or deranged) man, there is an even more remarkable woman. In this case, Mrs. Partridge, who runs their torture chamber with a motherly touch!

#28: "The Girls of Nazarone Affair" (4/12/65)
Written by Peter Barry
Lavinia Brown: Kipp Hamilton

GUEST CAST
Mme. Alceste Streigau: Marian Moses
Lucia Nazarone: Danica d'Hondt
Dr. Nicole Baurel: Ben Wright
Sophie: Kathy Kersh
Therapist: Sharon Tate

On the trail of a new and mysterious formula and its creator, Ilya and Solo encounter race car driver Lucia Nazarone, who is in league with Madame Streigau— until Steigau shoots Nazarone with a THRUSH weapon. Matters get complicated when Nazarone turns up alive and well. Our heroes learn that the formula increases the human metabolic rate. Nazarone was shot, but her body recovered. To top things off, Streigau turns out be old nemesis Dr. Egret, in her latest disguise.

#29: "The Odd Man Affair" (4/19/65)
Written by Dick Nelson
Directed by Joseph Sargent
GUEST CAST
Albert Sully: Martin Balsam
Bryn Watson: Barbara Shelley
Ecks: Christopher Cary
Wye: Hedley Mattingly
Zed: Ronald Long

A strange plot to unite Europe's right-wing and left-wing terrorists into a single force (go figure!) finally gets underway when the sole holdout, the terrorist Remond, blows

himself up in an airliner bathroom.
When U.N.C.L.E. gets a man named
Sully to impersonate Remond, the
plan almost works, until Sully does
not react to an enemy agent's cigarette smoke— Remond was allergic
to tobacco. A pin with a bomb on it
is planted on Sully, but Sully switch-
es it onto the mastermind of this evil
plan, and the villain succeeds in
blowing himself up instead.

Chapter Eighteen
Second Season

(In Color)

#30 and #31: "The Alexander The Greater Affair"—
 Part One (9/17/65) and Part Two (9/24/65)
Written by Dean Hargrove
Directed by Joseph Sargent
GUEST CAST
Alexander: Rip Torn
Tracey Alexander: Dorothy Provine
Parviz: David Sheiner

Our intrepid men from U.N.C.L.E. must defeat tycoon Alexander, who has stolen a mind-destroying chemical in his quest to break all ten commandments. Since this is television, the trick is to stop him before he gets to adultery! (For more details, see the chapter U.N.C.L.E. MOVIES.)

#32: "The Ultimate Computer Affair" (10/1/65)
Written by Peter Allen Fields
Directed by Joseph Sargent
GUEST CAST
Governor Callahan: Charlie Ruggles

Captain Cervantes: Roger C. Carmel
Salty Oliver: Judy Carne

Ilya infiltrates a South American prison colony the hard way, but with good reason. THRUSH is using it to develop a crime computer.

#33: "The Foxes and Hounds Affair" (10/8/65)
Written by Peter Fields
Directed by Alf Kjellin
GUEST CAST
Victor Martin: Vincent Price
Mimi Doolittle: Julie Sommers

Solo must distract THRUSH from another U.N.C.L.E. agent on a crucial mission. He doesn't know the set-up, which adds to the confusion on both sides of this deadly game.

#34: "The Discoteque Affair" (10/15/65)
Written by Dean Hargrove
Directed by Tom Gries
GUEST CAST
Vincent Carver: Ray Danton

Tiger Ed: Harvey Lembeck

THRUSH bugs the apartment next to Waverly's office! What kind of security does U.N.C.L.E. have, anyway?

#35: "The Re-Collectors Affair" (10/25/65)
Written by Alan Caillou
Directed by Alvin Ganzer
GUEST CAST
Demos: George Macready
Gregori Valetti: Theodore

The re-collectors are people who track down Nazi war criminals and kill them to re-collect the art treasures stolen by the Third Reich during World War Two. U.N.C.L.E. sends in its men to break up this deadly activity.

#36: "The Arabian Affair" (10/29/65)
Written by Peter Fields
Directed by E. Darrell Hallenbeck
GUEST CAST
Sophie: Phyllis Newman
Sulador: Michael Ansara
David: Robert Ellenstein

An important mission in the Mid-East goes haywire when Ilya is abducted by a sheik's daughter. She intends to trade in her new slave for an even newer camel!

#37: "The Tigers Are Coming Affair" (11/5/65)
Written by Alan Caillou
Director: Herschel Daugherty
GUEST CAST
Suzanne De Serre: Jill Ireland
Colonel Quillon: Alan Caillou

A crooked Indian ruler steals a new pesticide formula created by Suzanne De Serre, who calls in U.N.C.L.E. on the case.

#38: "The Deadly Toys Affair" (11/12/65)
Written by Robert Hill
Directed by John Brahm
GUEST CAST
Elfie Van Donck: Angela Lansbury
Bartlett: Jay North

Wacky actress Elfie Van Donck manages to keep both U.N.C.L.E. and THRUSH from locating her nephew, the child prodigy Bartlett Armand.

#39: "The Cherry Blossom Affair" (11/19/65)
Written by Mark Weingart
Directed by Joseph Sargent
GUEST CAST
Cricket Okasada: Frances Nguyen
Mr. Kutuzov: Woodrow Parfrey
Harada: Jerry H. Fujikawa

Things heat up in Japan when our heroes must find the Asian headquarters of THRUSH before a deadly new earthquake-inducing invention can be activated.

#40: "The Virtue Affair" (12/3/65)
Written by Henry Slesar
Directed by Jud Taylor
GUEST CAST
Robespiere: Ronald Long
Raoul Dubois: Marcel Hillaire
Albert: Mala Powers
Carl Voegler: Frank Marth

Robespierre is a politician with well-known views supporting conventional morality. This makes the fact that he's been kidnapping missile scientists all the more perplexing to Ilya and the lady scientist aiding him in this affair.

#41: "The Children's Day Affair" (12/10/65)
Written by Dean Hargrove
Directed by Sherman Marks
GUEST CAST
Mother Fear: Jeanne Cooper
Dennis Jenks: Warren Stevens
Anna Paola: Susan Silo

A secret U.N.C.L.E. conference in Switzerland has strange trouble with children. It seems that U.N.C.L.E. intelligence missed the fact that the conference location is perilously close to a boys' school run by— you guessed it— THRUSH!

#42: "The Adriatic Express Affair" (12/17/65)
Written by Robert Hill
Directed by Seymour Robbie
GUEST CAST
Madama Nemirovitch: Jessie Royce Landis
Eva: Juliet Mills

Our heroes are hot on the trail of a THRUSH agent carrying a deadly plague.

#43: "The Yukon Affair" (12/24/65)
Written by Marc Siegel
Directed by Alf Kjellin
GUEST CAST
Partridge: George Sanders
Murphy: Tianne Gabrielle
Victoria: Marion Thompson

U.N.C.L.E. foe Mr. Partridge, who has relocated in the far North, returns, and he's discovered a magnetic ore that can dirsupt all sea-faring navigational devices.

#44: "The Very Important Zombie Affair" (12/31/65)
Written by Boris Ingster
Directed by David Alexander
GUEST CAST
El Supremo: Claude Akins
Dr. Delgado: Ken Renard
Capt. Ramirez: Rodolfo Acosta
Suzy: Linda Gaye Scott
Mama Lou: Maidie Norman

It's voodoo time in the Caribbean, as our heroes must liberate a freedom fighter in the clutches of a voodoo-crazed despot cut from the Duvalier mold.

#45: "The Dippy Blonde Affair"
(1/7/66)
Written by Peter Allan Fields
Directed by E. Darrell Hallenbeck
GUEST CAST
Jojo Tyler: Joyce Jameson
Simon Belanado: Robert Strauss
Harry Pendleton: Fabrizio Mioni

Solo lucks out in more ways than one in his search for a THRUSH agent with yet another deadly device. It seems that this bad guy's girlfriend is more than willing to switch loyalties— for a price.

#46: "The Deadly Goddess Affair"
(1/14/66)
Written by Robert Hill
Directed by Seymour Robbie
GUEST CAST
Colonel Hubris: Victor Buono

A poverty-stricken Greek island seems to be the crash site of a THRUSH robot plane that had been carrying ten million dollars worth of stolen goods— which interests the locals just as much as it does U.N.C.L.E..

#47: "The Birds and Bees Affair"
(1/21/66)
Written by Mark Weingart
Directed by Alvin Ganzer
GUEST CAST
Mozart: John McGiver
Dr. Elias Swan: John Abbott
Tavia Sandor: Anna Capri

Years before SATURDAY NIGHT LIVE, Ilya and Solo encounter deadly killer bees. They are minute bees that can barely be seen with the naked eye have killed everyone in U.N.C.L.E.'s Swiss headquarters.

#48: "The Waverly Ring Affair"
(1/28/66)
Written by Jerry McNeely
Directed by John Brahm
GUEST CAST
George Donnell: Larry Blyden
Carla Drosten: Elizabeth Allen

Evidence is uncovered which reveals that a THRUSH agent has infiltrated U.N.C.L.E..

#49 and #50: "The Bridge of Lions Affair"—
Part One (2/4/66) and Part Two (2/11/66)
Written by Henry Slesar (story) and Howard Rodman (teleplay)
Directed by E. Darrell Hallenbeck
GUEST CAST
Sir Norman Swickert: Maurice Evans
Mme. Desala: Vera Miles

Jordan: Bernard Fox
Joanna Sweet: Ann Elder

THRUSH and U.N.C.L.E. face off in a contest to locate a rejuvenation serum and its creator.(For more details, see the chapter U.N.C.L.E. MOVIES.)

#51: "The Foreign Legion Affair" (2/18/66)
Written by Berne Giler
Directed by John Brahm
GUEST CAST
Captain Basil Calhoun: Howard da Silva
Barbara: Danielle DeMetz

When the pilot of his chartered plane turns out to be THRUSH agent, Ilya bails out, taking a stewardess with him. Stranded in the desert, they discover a forgotten outpost of the Foreign Legion, and recruit the Legionnaires in the battle against THRUSH.

#52: "The Moonglow Affair" (2/25/66)
Written by Dean Hargrove
Directed by Joseph Sargent
(Pilot for "The Girl From U.N.C.L.E." series)
GUEST CAST
April Dancer: Mary Ann Mobley
Mark Slate: Norman Fell
Arthur Caresse: Kevin McCarthy
Jean: Mary Carver

Solo and Ilya succumb to a new form of radiation, and will die in just two days— unless U.N.C.L.E. agent Mark Slate and his trainee April Dancer can find the antidote in time.

#53: "The Nowhere Affair" (3/4/66)
Written by Robert Hill
Directed by Michael Ritchie
GUEST CAST
Mara: Diana Hyland
Arum Tertunian: Lou Jacoby

Solo's mission to Nowhere, Nevada, turns up a dead THRUSH agent— and a clue to the secret THRUSH hideaway where computer scientist Tertunian is being held captive. Captured by THRUSH, Solo takes Capsule B, a special drug that eradicates his memory for three days! The head of THRUSH uses one of his female agents to "stimulate" Solo's memory, which doesn't quite work out: she falls in love with Solo!

#54: "The King of Diamonds Affair" (3/11/66)
Written by Edwin Blum and Leo Townsend
Directed by Joseph Sargent
GUEST CAST
Rafael Delgado: Ricardo Montalban
Victoria: Nancy Kovack

A stolen diamond in a package of pudding draws beautiful pudding heiress Victoria Pogue into a plot involving Solo, Ilya and world-class jewel thief Rafael Delgado (Ricardo Montalban). Bad guys with umbrella-guns (holy shades of the Penguin!) and henchmen with inappropriate accents add to the confusion of this silly outing, enhanced mainly by the sexy Nancy Kovack.

#55: "The 'Project Deephole' Affair" (3/18/66)
Written by Dean Hargrove
Directed by Alex March
GUEST CAST
Buzz Conway: Jack Weston
Narcissus Darling: Barbara Bouchet
Elom: Leon Askin
Leon: Tony Monaco
Dr. Remington: Ralph J. Rose
Manager: Walter Sande

THRUSH, planning to trigger earthquakes by drilling to the planet's core, tries to abduct Dr. Remington from Solo and Ilya— but botch the job and kidnap Buzz, a young homeless man, instead. Solo rescues Buzz and decides to use this confusion against THRUSH. Complicating matters is the fact that one of Solo's ex-girfriends is now working for THRUSH!

#56: "The Round Table Affair" (4/25/66)
Written by Robert Hill
Written by E. Darrell Hallenbeck
GUEST CAST
Vicky: Valura Noland
Lucha Nostra: Bruce Gordon
Artie King: Don Francks
Prince Fred: Reginald Gardiner
Doc: Stuart Nisbit
Bullets: Tom Barto
Herald: Eric Lord

Ilya chases a Mafia boss across Europe— until he crashes the border of Ingolstein, a tiny, unkown country that is a haven for crooks. Tossed in the slammer for destroying the border crossing, Ilya contacts Solo, who locates the real ruler of Ingolstein, Princess Vioctoria, in a French school— her U.N.C.L.E., the regent Freddie, is responsible for the state of things. On her return, Victoria begins to set up extradition treaties so that crooks can't take refuge in her country. When the Mafia don suggests that Freddie marry off his niece to jewel thief Artie King, things seem to be going badly for the forces of goodness— until Artie and the Princess really fall in love, and everything works out just fine.

#57: "The Bat Cave Affair" (5/1/66)
Written by Jerry McNeely
Directed by Alf Kjellin
GUEST CAST
Clemency McGill: Joan Freeman
Count Zark: Martin Landau
Professor Harvey Glomm: Whit Bissell
Transom: Peter Barone
Servant: Charles Horvath
U.N.C.L.E. Radio Man: Craig Shreeve
Flamenco Dancer: Tita Marshall

Cycle Repairman: Gene Roth

Claiming psychic powers, Clemency McGill clues Solo in to Ilya's predicament: he is in danger in Spain. This seems impossible, but it turns out that Ilya was diverted to Spain while on a mission to another country, kidnapped by THRUSH, and tossed into a bullring. Ilya escapes, but offends the bullfight fans with his unsportsmanlike conduct.

Solo joins him in Seville (the movie shown on his airplane is ONE SPY TOO MANY), where they encounter Count Zark, another THRUSH mastermind with a dire scheme up his sleeve— he intends to disrupt all air traffic unless THRUSH is paid a billion dollars. His plan involves bats which have been bred to interfere with aircraft radar. The Count, who lives in a crumbling castle, is a real Dracula type, with some trained vampire bats on hand as well. Clemency's psychic power turns out to be information broadcast by a THRUSH computer to a receiver in her hair!

#58: "The Minus X Affair" (5/8/66)
Written by Peter Allan Fields
Directed by Barry Shear
GUEST CAST
Professor Stemmler: Eve Arden
Leslie: Sharon Farrell
Rollo: Theo Marcuse
Whittaker: King Moody
Louis: Robert Doyle

Officer: John Bryant
Sergeant: Jan Peters
First M.P.: Paul Winfield

Captured by THRUSH, U.N.C.L.E. agent Louis escaps. He seems to have gone quite mad, along with having intensified senses. This resembles the effects expected from a drug in development, "Plus X," so our heroes visit "Plus X" inventor Professor Stemmler. They foil a robbery by THRUSH agents, and strive to protect Stemmler and her daughter Leslie.

A trumpet-playing THRUSH agents knocks out Ilya with a tranquilizer dart fired from his instrument, and kidnaps Leslie. This is all a ruse, anyway— Stemmler has been a THRUSH gaent all along. She has also created "Minus X," which basically destroys minds. But as the plot progresses, THRUSH threatens Leslie, and the Professor chooses to save her daughter, foiling THRUSH but losing her life in the process.

#59: "The Indian Affairs Affair" (5/15/66)
Written by Dean Hargrove
Directed by Alf Kjellin
GUEST CAST
Charisma: Angel Dorian
L.C. Carson: Joe Mantell
Chief Highcloud: Ted De Corsia
Dr. Yamaha: Richard Loo
Ralph: Nick Colasanto

THRUSH kidnaps an Indian chief and frames U.N.C.L.E., which results in a weird variety of Indian attacks on Solo and Ilya. They soon get to the bottom of this and wind up on an Indian reservation where THRUSH is trying to build a transistorized nuclear bomb devised by their Japanese division. Rather silly, but fun, with Ilya disguising himself as an Indian, and a role by a young Nick Colassanto, best known as Coach on CHEERS.

Chapter Nineteen
Third Season

#60: "Their Master's Voice Affair"
(9/16/66)
Written by Berne Giler
Directed by Barry Shear
GUEST CAST
Hester Partridge: Estelle Winwood
Jason Sutro: Joseph Ruskin
Verity Burgoyne: Marianne Osborne
Miki Matsu: Victoria Young
Dr. Matsu: Dale Ishimoto
Suzy: Cathy Ferrar
Dottie: Judy Franklin

GUEST CAST
Andy: Jeannie Riley
Margo: Pamela Curran
Dr. Pertwee: Woodrow Parfrey
Lash: Barry Atwater
Toffler: Fritz Feld
Analyst: William Lantau
A-77: Willy Koopman
Madame Hecubah: Naomi Stevens
U.N.C.L.E. Agent: Sharyn Hillyer
Zohmer: Jonathan Hole
Photographer: Nicky Blair

Miki, the daughter of a Japanese diplomat under U.N.C.L.E. protection, falls prey to a truly vile THRUSH plot: an ice-cream truck has hypnotized her with its music. Our heroes investigate Miki's all-girl school and uncover a plot, led by headmistress/THRUSH agent Miss Partridge, to brainwash the daughters of world leaders, many of whom board at her exclusive school.

Beautiful but deadly androids figure in Thrush's latest scheme. Can our heroes avoid being distracted by a beautiful bikini-clad model shooting a perfume commercial long enough to wrap up this crazy Ellison-penned affair?

#61: "The Sort Of Do-It-Yourself Dreadful Affair"
(9-23-66)
Written by Harlan Ellison
Directed by E. Darrell Hallenbeck

#62: "The Galatea Affair" (9/30/66)
Written by Jackson Gillis
Directed by E. Darrell Hallenbeck
GUEST CAST
Rosy Schlagenheimer/Bibi: Joan Collins
Slate: Noel Harrison

Baron De Chausser: Carl Esmond
Olaf: Michael St. Clair
American: Paul Smith
Thirty: Richard Angarola
Wine Steward: Chris Essay

Bibi is the wife of a Baron kidnapped by THRUSH, which forces her to act as their unwilling agent. Mark Slate teams with Ilya (Solo has pneumonia after a dunk in the canals of Venice— and Robert Vaughn was guesting on THE GIRL FROM U.N.C.L.E.) and hatches a scheme that will use Rosy, a perfect double of the Baroness— except for her thick Bronx accent.

Ilya replaces the Baroness' tennis teacher (I SPY, anyone?), but he is soon discovered when listening devices are found hidden in his rackets. The Baron, really a willing THRUSH man, plots to use his wife to replace Rosy, but decides to kill her, along with everyone else, when she falls for another man. All ends well, with the Baroness revealing all she knows about THRUSH, and Rosy finding a millionaire husband.

#63: "The Super-Collosal Affair" (10/7/66)
Written by Stanford Sherman
Directed by Barry Shear
GUEST CAST
Veblen: Shelly Berman
Ginger Laveer: Carol Wayne
Uncle Giuliano: J. Carrol Naish
Cariago: Bernard Fein
Angelo: Albert Shelly

Hardy Twill: John Bryant
Molcho: James Boles
Old Lady: Kathryn Minner
Process Server: John Harmon

Mobsters upset at the growing legitimization of Las Vegas plan to douse the city with a skunk bomb, driving all the tourists away for years to come. U.N.C.L.E. sends in our heroes to defuse this plot— but why? It sounds like a pretty good idea, if you really think about it.

#64: "The Monks of St. Thomas Affair" (10/14/66)
Written by Sheldon Stark
Directed by Alex March
GUEST CAST
Andrea Fouchet: Celeste Yarnall
Abbot Simon: David J. Stewart
Abbot John: John Wengraf
Brother Peter: Henry Calvin
Brother Paulus: Iggie Wolfington
Dolby: Horst Ebersberg
Prior: Roy Sickner
Wood Chopper: Ray Kellogg
Customs Man: Eugene Mate

Lambert, the inventor of a new laser component, is killed by THRUSH agents, who steal the device from his Felton Street home. Solo finds a bottle of a rare fine liquer in Lambert's lab, which is odd— the doctor did not drink alchohol. Waverly sends Solo to the Swiss monastery, where this liqueur is made, to investigate, and to bring a case back for Waverly.

Solo is turned back at the monastery door, but not before a talkative monk slips him a bottle with a message in it hinting at trouble in the monastery. Ilya's trail also leds him to Switzerland, where he recovers the laser part and then goes to help Solo liberate the monks from a THRUSH takeover of their mountain hideaway.

#65: "The Pop Art Affair" (10/21/66)
Written by John Shaner and Al Ramus
Directed by George Waggonner
GUEST CAST
Sylvia Harrison: Sherry Alberoni
Mari Brooks: Sabrina Scharf
Mark Ole: Robert Harris
Mrs. Harrison: Nellie Burt
Mr. Harrison: Charles Lane
Beatnik: Stanley Ralph Ross
Wanda: Sharon Hillyer
Espresso Man: Jack Perkins
Coplin: Tommy Farell
Dominic: Frederic Villani
Heidi: Lynn Carey

This is a complicated tale indeed. Ilya must pose as a beatnik to get the jump on Thrush's plan to develop a deadly new hiccup gas. (Think about it— it's a pretty horrible way to die!) Hip coffee shop scenery abounds, as does some pretty cool THRUSH weaponry: exploding golf balls and steel-tipped skateboards, all wielded by killer beatniks! Writer Stanley Ralph Ross, who scripted the next epsidoe as well as many BATMAN shows, plays one of the many semi-convincing beatniks in this outing, which is still pretty funny today.

#66: "The Thor Affair" (10/28/66)
Written by Don Richman and Stanley Ralph Ross
Directed by Sherman Marks
GUEST CAST
Thor: Bernard Fox
Dr. Frazir Nahdi: Harry Davis
Nellie Cranford: Linda Foster
Mohan Kiru: Arthur Batanides
Dr. Diljohn: Ken Renard
Clerk: Charles Giorgi
Butler: Anthony Eustrel
Hotel Clerk: R. Traeger

Indian president Nahdi vows to stage a hunger strike until the world powers disarm. A peace conference is set in Geneva, so Nahdi ends his fast and goes there, narrowly avoiding an assassin's bullet when a passing cat makes him sneeze. Our heroes are sent to protect him, only to have Solo's suitcase boobytrapped by the assassin, Kiru.

American toursit Nellie Canford saves the day when her fillings pick up the radio transmissions directed at Kiru, and she throws the suitcase out the window just in time. The man behind all this is munitions magnate Thor, who has a new plan to get Nahdi— the last page of Nahdi's speech is treated to trigger Nahdi's feline allergy, and Nahdi's handkerchief is treated to explode on contact with any liquid!

#67: "The Candidate's Wife Affair" (11/4/66)
Written by Robert Hill
Directed by George Waggner
GUEST CAST
Miranda Bryant/Irina: Diana Hyland
Senator Bryant: Richard Anderson
Fairbanks: Larry D. Mann

THRUSH scores another coup for evil when it abducts the wife of a presidential candidate and replaces her with a duplicate— can our men from U.N.C.L.E. undo the damage of this heinous crime before THRUSH gets a foothold in the White House.

#68: "The Come With Me To The Casbah Affair" (11/11/66)
Written by Robert Hill
From a story by Robert Hill, Danielle Branton and Norman Lenzer
Directed by E. Darrell Hallenbeck
GUEST CAST
Janine: Danielle DeMetz
Pierrot La Mouche: Pat Harrington
Col. Hamid: Jacques Aubuchon

A million francs is all that the crooked LaMouche wants for a THRUSH codebook he has obtained— that and the companionship of the lovely Janine. U.N.C.L.E. must find away to win their prize without pandering to LaMouche's insidious desires.

#69: "The Off-Broadway Affair" (11/18/66)
Written by Jerry McNeely
Directed by Sherman Marks
GUEST CAST
Janet Jarrod: Shari Lewis

Ilya, who has already performed bad beatnik poetry a few episodes back, now must tread the boards in an Off-Broadway musical when U.N.C.L.E. tracks a THRUSH plot to an off-the-wall theater.

#70: "The Concrete Overcoat Affair, Part One" (11/25/66)
Written by Peter Allen Fields and David Victor
Directed by Joseph Sargent
GUEST CAST
Louis Strago: Jack Palance
Miss Diketon: Janet Leigh
Fingers: Eduardo Cianelli
Pia Monteri: Letitia Roman
Enzo Stilletto: Allen Jenkins

This time around, Thrush's plan is particularly grandiose: they intend to divert the Gulf Stream. Solo and Ilya encounter a beautiful Sicilian girl and her Mafia family in the course of their investigation.

#71: "The Concrete Overcoat Affair, Part Two" (12/2/66)
Written by Peter Allen Fields and David Victor
Directed by Joseph Sargent
GUEST CAST
Louis Strago: Jack Palance
Miss Diketon: Janet Leigh
Fingers: Eduardo Cianelli
Pia Monteri: Letitia Roman
Enzo Stilletto: Allen Jenkins

Ilya and Pia Monteri are prisoners of THRUSH— and Solo must enlist the aid of the notorious Stiletto brothers in liberating them. (For more details, see the chapter U.N.C.L.E. MOVIES.)

#72: "The Abominable Snowman Affair" (12/9/66)
Written by Krishna Shah
Directed by Otto Lang
GUEST CAST
Prime Minister: David Sheiner
Calamith Rogers: Anne Jeffrys
Amra Palli: Pilar Seurat
Baku: Stewart Hsieh
High Lama: Philip Ahn

The security of a strategically located Himalayan nation is threatened when the evil prime minister plots to replace the venerable High Lama with his own crooked son.

#73: "The My Friend The Gorilla Affair" (12/16/66)

Written by Don Richman and Joseph Sandy
Directed by Alex Singer
GUEST CAST
Girl: Vitina Marcus
Harry Blackburn: Alan Mowbray
Marsha Woodhugh: Joyce Jillson
Khufu: Percy Rodriguez
Arunda: Ray St. Jacques

Where's Tarzan when you need him? Solo and Ilya confront an evil African witch doctor in a tale that also involves big game hunters, a jungle woman with a tame gorilla, dying elephants and the obligatory killer ants.

#74: "The Jingle Bells Affair" (12/23/66)
Written by William Fay
Directed by John Brahm
GUEST CAST
Emissary Georgi Koz: Akim Tamiroff
Priscilla: Ellen Willard
Maxim Radish: Leon Belasco
Ferenc Pifnic: Leonid Kinskey

In this Christmas episode, Solo, Ilya and Salvation Army girl Priscilla Worth must invoke the true spirit of the season to defuse an angry Soviet official who's just mad enough to trigger a global conflict.

#75: "The Take Me To Your Leader Affair" (12/30/66)
Written by Berne Giler
Directed by George Waggner

GUEST CAST
Coco: Nancy Sinatra
Corinne: Whitney Blake
Sparrow: Paul Lambert
Dr. Adrian Cool: Woodrow Parfrey
Dr. Trebush: James Griffith

Nancy Sinatra stars as Coco, who is kidnapped by the evil Simon Sparrow. It seems that Sparrow has an unusual ransom demand: Coco's father is a famous astronomer, and Sparrow wants him to announce an alien invasion, news that will create worldwide panic and allow Sparrow to take over just about everything.

#76: "The Suburbia Affair" (12/30/66)
Written by Sheridan Gibney and Stanford Sherman
Directed by Charles Haas
GUEST CAST
Dr. Rutters/Willoughby: Victor Borge
Betsy: Beth Brickell
P.T. Barkley: Richard Erdman
Miss Witherspoon: Rita Shaw

Now THRUSH is trying to get their evil clutches on an anti-matter formula, created by a scientist who is hiding out in a peaceful, boring suburban community which is about to become the latest field of battle between the evil organization and their arch-enemies, U.N.C.L.E..

#77: "The Deadly Smorgasbord Affair" (1/6/67)
Written by Stanley Ross and Peter Bourne
Directed by Barry Shear
GUEST CAST
Neilla: Lynn Loring
Inga Anderson: Pamela Curran
Heinrich Beckman: Robert Emhardt
Dr. A.C. Nillson: Peter Brocco

Thrush's Swedish branch, well acquainted with colder climates, has hatched a scheme to put U.N.C.L.E. on ice permanently— with a new technique of suspended animation.

#78: "The Yo-Ho-Ho And A Bottle Of Rum Affair" (1/20/67)
Written by Norman Hudis
Directed by E. Darrell Hallenbeck
GUEST CAST
Captain Morton: Dan O'Herlihy
Passenger: Kevin Hagen
Jenny Janue: Peggy Taylor
Scotty: Eddin Quillan

In a scenario predating the Exxon Valdez disaster, THRUSH sets a new tidal-wave device to sea on a ship whose captain is a tough, booze-drinking bad guy more than ready to give Ilya a run for his money.

#79: "The Napoleon's Tomb Affair" (1/27/67)
Written by James N. Whiton
Directed by John Brahm

GUEST CAST
President Tunick: Kurt Kasznar
Malanez: Joseph Sirola
Edgar: Ted Cassidy
Banker/Beatnik/Waiter/Diplomat:
Fritz Feld

A plan to steal Napoleon Bonaparte's coffin (and presumably Napoleon as well) is just part of the dastardly goings-on, in Paris this time out.

#80: "The It's All Greek To Me Affair" (2/3/67)
Written by Robert Hill and Erich Faust
Directed by George Waggner
GUEST CAST
Stauros: Harold J. Stone
Kyra: Linda Marsh
Manolakas: George Keymas
Nico: Ted Roter

A routine search for a missing codebook gets complicated in Greece when a Greek bandit mistakes Solo and Ilya for THRUSH agents— and does everything in his power to get in their way.

#81: "The Hula Doll Affair" (2/17/67)
Written by Stanford Sherman
Directed by Eddie Saeta
GUEST CAST
Simos Sweet: Jan Murray
Peter Sweet: Pat Harrington
Mama Sweet: Patsy Kelly

Wendy Thyme: Grace Gaynor
Oregano: Rex Holman

A struggle over a new explosive is complicated by the duelling Sweet brothers, both of whom are vying for the position of Thrush's New York chief. Solo is forced to impersonate THRUSH agent #26 by one brother— but the real agent #26 is their mother. The hula doll of the title contains a sample of the explosive, which will explode at 90 degrees Farenheit, and New York is in the middle of a heat wave! (Interestingly enough, the entrance to THRUSH's New York hideout is through a men's clothing shop.)

#82: "The Pieces of Fate Affair" (2/24/67)
Written by Harlan Ellison (with Yale Urdoff)
Directed by John Brahm
GUEST CAST
Jacqueline Midcult: Sharon Farrell
Jody Moore (originally Judith Merle): Grayson Hill
Ellipsis Zark: Theodore Marcuse
Uncle Charlie: Charles See

When U.N.C.L.E. ralizes that a new bestseller by Jacqueline Midcult is based on information from some missing THRUSH diaries, it's a race to see who gets the information from her on where the diaries are now. The problem is that Jacquelin Midcult has lost her memory following a THRUSH attempt on her life and Solo and Illya must take her to a relative's home to try and jog her memory. THRUSH is not far behind, and the codebooks are closer than anyone realizes.

#83: "The Matterhorn Affair" (3/3/67)
Written by David Giler
Directed by Bill Finnegan
GUEST CAST
Klump: Bill Dana
Heather Klump: Norma Chase
Backstreet: Oscar Boreg
Beirut: Vito Scotti

The battle for a miniature nuclear reactor takes Solo and Ilya from Singapore to Southern California to the Matterhorn (the real one, not the Disney ride), with nebbishy Marvin Klump along for the ride.

#84: "The Hot Number Affair" (3/10/67)
Written by Joseph and Carol Cavella
Directed by George Waggner
GUEST CAST
Jerry: Sonny
Ramona: Cher
Harry Parkington: George Tobias
Harry Sighn: Ned Glass

A piece of cloth with a secret THRUSH report sewn into it makes its way to a small fashion business, where Sonny and Cher both work!

#85: "The When In Rome Affair" (3/17/67)
Written by Gloria Elmore
Directed by George Waggner
GUEST CAST
Darlene Sims: Julie Sommars
Cesare Guardia: Cesare Danova

Once again, an attractive American tourist is drawn into the fray when Solo, pursued by THRUSH agents in Rome, drops a perfume spray containing a secret formula into her purse.

#86: "The Apple-A-Day Affair" (3/24/67)
Written by Joe Cavella and Lee Roberts
Directed by E. Darrell Hallenbeck
GUEST CAST
Colonel Picks: Robert Emhardt
Nina Lillette: Jeannie Riley

Exploding apples, hillbilly hijinks and a shotgun wedding involving Solo make up the bulk of this silly episode.

#87: "The Five Daughters Affair, Part One" (3/31/67)
Written by Norman Hudis and Boris Ingster
Directed by Barry Shear
GUEST CAST
Amanda: Joan Crawford
Carl Von Kesser: Curt Jergens
Count Fanzini: Telly Savalas
Constable: Terry-Thomas
Randolph: Herbert Lom

Sandy True: Kim Darby
Margo: Diane McBain
Imogene: Jill Ireland
Yvonne: Danielle DeMetz
Reikko: Irene Tsu
Sazami Kyushn: Philip Ahn

When Dr. True, inventor of a process to extract gold from sea water, is killed by THRUSH, Solo's only clue leads him to search for True's daughters.

#88: "The Five Daughters Affair, Part Two" (4/7/67)
Written by Norman Hudis and Boris Ingster
Directed by Barry Shear

The conclusion. (For more details, see the chapter U.N.C.L.E. MOVIES.)

#89: "The Cap and Gown Affair" (4/14/67)
Written by Stanford Sherman
Directed by George Waggner
GUEST CAST
Timothy Dwight: Henry Jones
Minerva Dwight: Carole Shelyne
Jonathan Trumble: Larry Mann
Gregory Haymish: Zalman King

Waverly must avoid exposure until THRUSH relents in its present quest to assassinate him— but on the other hand, he must appear at his alma mater to receive an honorary degree.

Chapter Twenty
Fourth Season

#90: "The Summit-Five Affair"
(9/11/67)
Written by Robert E. Thompson
Directed by Sutton Roley
GUEST CAST
Heinz Newman: Don Chastain
Gerald Strothers: Lloyd Bochner
Harry Beldon: Albert Decker
Helga Deniken: Susanne Cramer

Solo is framed, and must travel to East Germany to unravel the scheme that has implicated him as a THRUSH double agent.

#91: "The Test-Tube Killer Affair"
(9/18/67)
Written by Jack Turley
Directed by E. Darrell Hallenbeck
GUEST CAST
Greg Martin: Christopher Jones
Christine Hobson: Lynn Loring
Dr. Stroller: Paul Lukas

THRUSH has bred a genetically superior teenager with awesome powers and unleashed him on a Greek village. Solo and Ilya are pretty much out of their league in this affair!

#92: "The 'J' For Judas Affair"
(9/25/67)
Written by Norman Hudis
Directed by Alf Kjellin
GUEST CAST
Mark Tenza: Broderick Crawford
Adam Tenza: Chad Everett
Olivia: Delphi Laurence
"J": Claude Woolman
Darien: K. Hagen

Who is J? Inquiring minds want to know. So do Solo and Ilya, since this information is the only thing that can possibly stop the assassination of a rich industrialist and his son.

#93 and #94: "The Price Of Darkness Affair"—
Part One (10/2/67) and Part Two (10/9/67).
Written by Dean Hargrove
Directed by Boris Sagal
GUEST CAST
Luther Sebastian: Bradford Dillman
Parviz Kharmusi: John Dehner
Annie Justin: Carol Lynley
Azalea: Lola Albright

Luther Sebastian plans to unleash thermal destruction on the world from his desert hideaway. (For more details, see the chapter U.N.C.L.E. MOVIES.)

#95: "The Master's Touch Affair" (10/16/67)
Written by Boris Sobelman
Directed by John Brahm
GUEST CAST
Pharos: Jack Lord
Stephan Valandros: Nehemiah Persoff
Leslie Welling: Leslie Parrish

Looking suspiciouly like the star of HAWAII FIVE-O, THRUSH turncoat Pharos offers to sell U.N.C.L.E. a list of Thrush's top operatives. But his price is a bit too steep. He wants U.N.C.L.E. to kill someone for him!

#96: "The THRUSH Roulette Affair" (10/23/67)
Written by Arthur Weingarten
Directed by Sherman Marks
GUEST CAST
Barnaby Partridge: Michael Rennie
Taggart Coleman: Charles Drake
Monica: Nobu McCarthy

Set in a casino, this tale involves gambling, intrigue and world leaders who are dropping like flies.

#97: "The Deadly Quest Affair" (10/30/67)

Written by Robert E. Thompson
Directed by Alf Kjellin
GUEST CAST
Karmak: Darren McGavin
Sheila: Marlyn Mason
Stephan: T. Carey

Solo and a beautiful woman must locate Ilya in a devastated slum slated for razing, all the while being stalked by a crazed villain with a pet cheetah. THE MOST DANGEROUS game, this ain't!

#98: "The Fiery Angel Affair" (11/6/67)
Written by John W. Bloch
Directed by Richard Benedict
GUEST CAST
Angela Abaca: Madlyn Rhue
Paco: Joseph Sirola
Carlos Abaca: Perry Lopez
Vinay: Victor Lundin
Martine: Rudolpho Hoyos

Ilya foils a murder attempt on the popular female leader of a South American country, but is thrown in jail with the asassin. He is saved when the leader, Angela, gets him out of jail. Now he is a hero, which makes him a public figure, so Solo comes in to do the secret work. The quest for the Secret Three, who plan a coup, begins, and leads to the real culprit: Angela's military husband, who wants her out of the way. He is defeated, and democracy is restored.

#99: "The Survival School Affair" (11/20/67)
Written by Don Brinkley and Jack Turley
Directed by Charles Rondeau
GUEST CAST
John Saimes: Chris Robinson
Harry Williams: Richard beymer
Jules Cutter: Charles McGrew
Melissa Hargrove: Susan Odin

THRUSH has infiltrated U.N.C.L.E.'s island training camp, and a trainee turns up dead. Ilya is sent to investigate and uncover the double agent. If this mole cannot be found, the entire class will fail their courses, and all will be fired. Waverly isn't taking any chances. The trail leads to the three trainees most likely to flunk anyway. Why else would one of them turn traitor?

#100: "The Gurnius Affair" (11/27/67)
Written by Milton S. Gelman
Directed by Barry Shear
GUEST CAST
Zorcan Gurnius: George MacReady
Terry Cook: Judy Carne
Dr. Hans Van Etske: Will Kuluva
Brown: Joseph Ruskin
Technician: Frank Arno

Will Kuluva, who played original U.N.C.L.E. chief Mr. Allsion in the SOLO/U.N.C.L.E. pilot, finally gets on the show as Dr. Von Etske, a Nazi war criminal. Solo and Ilya travel to Germany to foil a rumored escape plot, but the Doctor gets away anyway. Fortunately, a Nazi agent killed in the aftermath of the breakout looks exactly like Ilya, which makes infiltration easy. The trail leads to South America, where THRUSH has teamed with Nazi baddie Gurnius, the Doctor's accomplice. The plot is foiled, but not before Ilya must pretend to torture Solo.

#101: "The Man From THRUSH Affair" (12/4/67)
Written by Robert I. Holt
Directed by James Sheldon
GUEST CAST
Dr. Killman: John Larch
Marnya: Barbara Luna
Andreas Petros: Robert Wolders
Marius: Mario Alcalde

Ilya sits out this episode, leaving Solo to team with with Greek U.N.C.L.E. agent Andreas Petros in another Mediterrannean adventure that finds them trying to discover what it is that THRUSH is up to on the isle of Irbos. Solo takes the place of a dead THRUSH agent and infiltrates a secret base while Petros falls in with the local workers— together they discover another THRUSH plot to trigger disastrous earthquakes around the world.

#102: "The Maze Affair" (12/18/67)
Written by Leonard Stadd

Directed by John Brahm
GUEST CAST
Dr. James Fabray: William Marshall
Abbe: Anna Capri
Barnes: Laurence Montaigne
Clemons: Barry Cahill
Old Man: Ralph Moody

THRUSH tests U.N.C.L.E.'s defenses by putting a bomb in a suit left for cleaning at Del Floria's tailor shop, but the scheme fails. No matter, they have their eyes on a new gun that destroys by disrupting its target on a molecular level! Solo falls victim to this device and is left for dead by the bad guys, but in fact the weapon has malfunctioned, and Solo survives to foil yet another THRUSH undertaking.

#103: "The Deep Six Affair" (12/25/67)
Written by Leonard Stadd
Directed by E. Darrell Hallenbeck
GUEST CAST
Commander Kohler: Alfred Ryder
Laura Adams: Diana Van Der Vlis
Brian Morton: Peter Bromilow
Mr. Yu: Dale Ishimoto
Submarine Captain: Gil Stuart
Uniformed Guard: Peter Forster
Miss Walker: Gay Hartwig

The MacGuffin this time around is a new model of submarine which THRUSH renegade Captain Krohler offers to U.N.C.L.E.— for a price. Krohler gets an edge over retiring

U.N.C.L.E. agent Brian Morton by kidnapping his fiancée, Laura. Turned double agent against his will, Morton winds up between a rock and a hard place when Solo and Ilya get into the action.

#104 and #105: "The Seven Wonders Of The World Affair"—
Part One (1/8/68) and Part Two (1/15/68)
Written by Norman Hudis
Directed by Sutton Riley
GUEST CAST
Maximilian Harmon: Leslie Nielsen
Mr. Webb: Mark Richman
Margitta Kingsley: Eleanor Parker
Robert Kingsley: Barry Sullivan
Prof. Garrow: Dan O'Herlihy
Steve Garrow: Tony Bill

The final story is classic U.N.C.L.E. all the way with suspense, humor, violence and a plot by THRUSH to completely take over the world with a gas which turns people into compliant servants.

In part one, scientists who are the foremost specialists in their field are being captured from disparate sites around the world. When U.N.C.L.E. determines that Prof. David Garrow is the next target, they watch what happens and follow him when he's kidnapped.

In part two Solo and Illya track Prof. Garrow to a secret base in a Shangri-La like valley in the Himalaya mountains. There they have their showdown with THRUSH

over the future of humanity, but not
without the tragic death of an innocent player.

Chapter Twentyone

The Girl from U.N.C.L.E.

Producer: Douglas Benton
Executive Producer: David Victor
Music: Richard Shores, David Grusin, Jeff Alexander
Theme: Jerry Goldsmith
Director of Photography: Harkness Smith
An Arena Production in association with MGM TV

    W = writer   D = director

Regular Cast
April Dancer: Stefanie Powers
Mark Slate: Noel Harrison
Mr. Waverly: Leo G. Carroll
Randy Kovacs: Randy Kirby (semi-regular)

#1: "The Dog-Gone Affair"
W: Tony Barrett
D: Barry Shear
GUEST CAST
Apollo Zakinthlos: Kurt Kasznar
Tuesday Hajadakis: Luciana Paluzzi
Antoine Fromage: Marcel Hillaire
Patras: Jan Arvan

Mark Slate, on an island where THRUSH is developing a devilish new drug, receives a package from April—a dachshund named Putzi whose fleas carry the drug's only antidote.

#2: "The Prisoner of Zalamar Affair"
W: Max Hodge
D: Herschel Daugherty
GUEST CAST
Vizier: Michael Ansara
Gizella: Brenda Benet
Omar: Abraham Sofer
Prince Ahmed: John Gabriel
Abou: Rafael Campos
Sheik Ali Hassen: Henry Calvin

April masquerades as Princess Fatima, a missing heiress to the throne of an oil-rich Zalamar in an attempt to forestall a takeover by Fatima's uncle, the evil grand vizier.

#3: "The Mother Muffin Affair"
W: Joseph Calvelli
D. Sherman Marks
GUEST CAST
Mother Muffin: Boris Karloff
Napoleon Solo: Robert Vaughn
Rodney Babcock: Bernard Fox

Vito Pomade: Bruce Gordon

In London, April and Napoleon Solo are ordered to return a gangster's daughter to the United States, but they are trapped in their hotel by the lovably murderous Mother Muffin and her assassin school pupils.

#4: "The Mata Hari Affair"
W: Samuel Peeples
D: Joseph Sargent
GUEST CAST
Sir Terrance Keats: Edward Mulhare
Mandy Dean Tanner: Jocelyn Lane
Toby Gordon-Jones: Christopher Cary

April assumes the identity of a murdered exotic dancer to force the killer to strike again and thereby expose himself.

#5: "The Montori Device Affair"
W: Boris Sobelman
D: John Brahm
GUEST CAST
Brassano: Edward Andrews
Prof. Boris Budge: John Carradine
Tullio: Ted Cassidy
Chu-Chu: Dee Hartford

U.N.C.L.E.'s communications network will be destroyed unless April can retrieve a device which has fallen into the hands of a fashion model employed by Conrad Brassano, a suspected THRUSH agent.

#6: "The Horns-of-the-Dilemma Affair"
W: Tony Barrett
D: John Brahm
GUEST CAST
Alejandro DeSada: Fernando Lamas
Paco: Alejandro Rey

In Mexico, April bluffs her way into a THRUSH bull ranch to locate three missing rocketry experts.

#7: "The Danish Blue Affair"
W: Arthur Weingarten
D: Mitchell Leisen
GUEST CAST
Stanley: Dom De Luise
Ole Bargman: Lloyd Bochner
Ingo: William Bramley
Granny: Virginia Gregg
Hansel: Mark De Vries
Gretel: Cindy Taylor
Prof. Voltan: Ivan Triesault
Chef: Fritz Feld

April and Mark compete with THRUSH to recover top-secret micro-dot blueprints hidden in a piece of cheese which was accidentally eaten by bumbling Stanley Umlaut.

#8: "The Garden of Evil Affair"
W: John O'Dea & Arthur Rowe
D: Jud Taylor

GUEST CAST
Iman Abbas: Arnold Moss
Brunhilde: Anna-Lisa
Miss Karem: Lisa Seagram
Greta Wolf: Sabrina Scharf
Hugo Von Gerb: Oscar Beregi
Duke Cornwallis: Patrick Horgan
THRUSH Director: Khigh Dhiegh

April and Mark try to beat THRUSH to a devilish serum which has been stolen by a Middle Eastern assassination cult.

#9: "The Atlantis Affair"
W: Richard Matheson
D: E. Darrell Hallenbeck
GUEST CAST
Prof. Henry Antrum: Sidney Blackmer
Vic Ryan: Denny Miller

In search of a cache of deadly crystals supposedly found on the lost continent of Atlantis, April and Mark travel to a 17th century plantation in Central America to battle the 20th century THRUSH.

#10: "The Paradise Lost Affair"
W: John O'Dea & Arthur Rowe
D: Alf Kjellin
GUEST CAST
Gomez: Monty Landis
Liverpool 'Enry: Chips Rafferty
Big Feets Charley: Raymond St. Jacques
Mme. Chop Chop: Mokihana

While trying to thwart a THRUSH smuggling operation, April and Mark are shipwrecked on an island ruled by Genghis Gomez III, a murderous monarch who considers such trespassing punishable by death.

#11: "The Lethal Eagle Affair"
W: Robert Hill
D: John Brahm
GUEST CAST
Gita: Margaret Leighton
Franz-Joseph: Michael Wilding
Dieter: Brian Avery

THRUSH retiree Gita Volander is making her comeback with her diabolical matter transmitter which Mark and April must seize before it is utilized on a human being.

#12: "The Romany Lie Affair"
W: Tony Barrett
D: Richard C. Sarafian
GUEST CAST
Sadvaricci: Lloyd Bochner
Mama Rosha: Gladys Cooper
Ponthea: Anna Mizrahi

April tries to capture a gypsy circus owner named Sadvaricci who's figured out a novel way to manipulate the European stock market by wooing and murdering wealthy women investors.

#13: "The Little John Doe Affair"
W: Joseph Calvelli
D: Leo Penn
GUEST CAST
Little John: Wally Cox
Joey Celeste: Pernell Roberts

April flies to Italy to protect an informer from underworld assassin and mild-mannered family man Little John Doe.

#14: "The Jewels of Topango Affair"
W: Berne Giler
D: John Brahm
GUEST CAST
Natasha: Lesli Uggams
King M'Bala: Brook Peters
Dr. Elmer Spritzer: John Qualen
Prince Nicholas: Booker Bradshaw
Whiteside: Barry Kalley
Byron Cavendish: Patrick Horgan

Natasha Brimstone, a fake U.N.C.L.E. agent, is part of a plot to rob the treasury of a diamond-rich African nation.

#15: "The Faustus Affair"
W: Jerry McNeely
D: Barry Shear
GUEST CAST
B. Elzie Bubb: Raymond Massey
Quantum: Tom Bosley
Goethe: Dick Crockett

Angelic April intercedes to save scrambled egghead Jonathan

Quantum from his pact with the satanic B. Elzie Bubb.

#16: "The U.F.O. Affair"
W. Warren Duff
D: Barry Shear
GUEST CAST
Salim Ibn Hydari: Fernando Lamas
Madame: Joan Blondell
Nur: Janet MacLachlan
Amintore Possetti: Anthony Caruso
aide: James Millhollin
guard: Lee Kolima
handmaiden: J. Clements

April goes undercover in a harum in North Africa to investigate a crime syndicate's caper involving an unidentified flying object.

#17: "The Moulin Ruse Affair"
W: Jay Simms and Fred Eggers
D: Barry Shear
GUEST CAST
Dr. Toulouse: Shelly Berman
Nadia Marcolescu: Yvonne DeCarlo
Mme. Bloor: Ellen Corby

April and Mark head for the Caribbean health spa of Dr. Toulouse. The pint-sized blackmailer threatens to sell his super-strength pill to THRUSH unless U.N.C.L.E. pays him five million dollars.

#18: "The Catacombs and Dogma Affair"
W: Warren Duff

D: E. Darrell Hallenbeck
GUEST CAST
Prince Boriarsi: Eduardo Cianelli
Cesare Boriarsi: Fabrizio Mioni
Adriana Raffaelli: Danielle DeMetz
Dossetti: Gerald Mohr
Hugo Horsch: Peter Marcus

April and Mark become involved in a plot to plunder the Vatican treasury by a self-styled 14th century Renaissance prince.

#19: "The Drublegratz Affair"
W: Boris Sobelman
D: Mitchell Leisen
GUEST CAST
Princess Rapunzel: Patricia Barry
Dr. Igor Gork: Vito Scotti
Sherilee: Jill Townsend
Prince Efrem: Christopher Held
the band: the Daily Flash

April and Mark join a rock and roll band to protect Prince Efrem, the swinging heir apparent to a Tyrolian throne.

#20: "The Fountain of Youth Affair"
W: Richard Deroy & Robert Bloch
D: Darrell Hallenbeck
GUEST CAST
Baroness: Gena Rowlands
Peter Starker: Dennelly Rhodes
Premier Dao: Philip Ahn
Mme. Dao: Miiko Taka
Charles Vechten: Gene Raymond

April and Mark must dry up a dangerous fountain of youth where Baroness Ingrid Blangsted is offering world leaders' wives rejuvination in return for shares in world power.

#21: "The Carpathian Caper Affair"
W: Arthur Weingarten
D: Barry Shear
GUEST CAST
Mother Magda: Ann Sothern
Herbert Fummer: Stan Freberg
Shirley Fummer: Joyce Jameson
Rock Munnis: Jack Cassidy
Miklos: George Furth
Papa: Bobby Gilbert

A pair of newlyweds are swept up in a search for a list of THRUSH operatives at a Carpathian borscht-circuit hotel. Obstacles include explosive golf balls and a gigantic pop-up toaster for people.

#22: The Furnace Flats Affair"
W: Archie Tegland
D: John Brahm
GUEST CAST
Packer Jo: Peggy Lee
Dolly X: Ruth Roman
Ladybug: Susan Browning
Asterick: Herb Edelman
Mesquite Swede: Percy Helton

A three woman race through Death Valley for a mineral which can turn laser light into a death ray involves U.N.C.L.E.'s April,

THRUSH's Dolly X and a longshot
named Ladybug Byrd.

#23: "The Low Blue C Affair"
W: Berne & David Giler
D: Barry Shear
GUEST CAST
Major Stella: Hermione Gingold
Soyil Irosian: Broderick Crawford
diplomat: Renzo Cesana
Dwayne: Stanley Clements

April must persuade a soul-sav-
ing woman crusader to redeem a
gambling-rich dukedom to which
she is heir, and disuade her gangster
cousin from killing her for the
throne.

#24: "The Petit Prix Affair"
W: Robert Hill
D: Mitchell Leisen
GUEST CAST
Desiree d'Oeuf: Nanette Fabray
Prof. Pamplemousee: Marcel Hillaire
Jean: Steve Harmon
Octave d'Oeuf: Michael Shillo

April and Mark plunge into a
high speed motor cart race in France
to try to prevent an armored car robbery to occur en route.